# LIVING *the*
# WORDS
*of* # JESUS

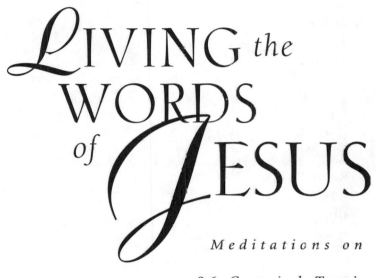

# LIVING *the* WORDS *of* JESUS

*Meditations on*

*96 Crucial Topics*

*of the*

*Christian Life*

# Rosemary Jensen

Kregel
*Publications*

*Living the Words of Jesus: Meditations on 96 Crucial Topics of the Christian Life*

© 2003 by Rosemary Jensen

Published by Kregel Publications, P.O. Box 2607, Grand Rapids, MI 49501.

Unless otherwise quoted, Scripture quotations are from the *Holy Bible, New International Version®.* © 1973, 1978, 1984 by International Bible Society. Used by permission of Zondervan Publishing House. All rights reserved.

Scripture quotations marked NRSV are from the New Revised Standard Version of the Bible, © 1989 by the Division of Christian Education of the National Council of the Churches of Christ in the USA. Used by permission.

**Library of Congress Cataloging-in-Publication Data**
Jensen, Rosemary.
   Living the words of Jesus: meditations on 96 crucial topics of the Christian life / by Rosemary Jensen.
      p. cm.
   1. Christian life—Meditations. I. Title

BV4501.3.J37 2003
248.4—dc21
2003001782

ISBN 0-8254-2943-9

Printed in the United States of America

03 04 05 06 07 / 5 4 3 2 1

# CONTENTS

# CONTENTS

# CONTENTS

# CONTENTS

# FOREWORD

*W*riting a foreword is like putting wrapping paper on a gift; it should entice the reader to open the book and discover the gift inside. As her pastor and friend of many years, it is my pleasure and honor to write this foreword for author Rosemary Jensen because her book is truly a gift to God's people. Peter wrote to Christians who never knew Jesus while He was on earth: "Though you have not seen him, you love him" (1 Peter 1:8). As those who have been regenerated by the Holy Spirit, Christians do love Jesus Christ; it is our new nature to do so. Yet, we must love Jesus on His terms, not ours. We must love Jesus as He commands, not as we think fitting. Christ told us precisely how we should love Him in John 14:15, "If you love me, you will keep my commandments" (NRSV). Still, how can we keep Christ's commandments if we do not know them? It is to this end that *Living the Words of Jesus* is made available, for when we know Jesus' teaching on a subject, we have the final word from Him who is the "Truth" (John 14:6). After all, Christians do "have the mind of Christ" (1 Corinthians 2:16).

Rosemary Jensen is no ivory-tower theologian who never gets her hands dirty with the grit and grime of real-life ministry. This book is written by someone who has lived in the trenches for decades as a servant of Christ, taking God's Word to the hurting and needy. For over twenty years Rosemary was the executive director of Bible Study Fellowship International, an organization that seeks to equip people with biblical truth so they can apply it to real-life situations. In addition, for over fifteen years she has headed the Rafiki Foundation, a missionary agency that demonstrates true and undefiled religion by taking Christ's gospel around the world to widows and orphans in their distress, while ministering to their physical needs as well.

*Living the Words of Jesus* was not written by a person who sat down to learn Christ's truth merely to instruct God's people. Rather, Rosemary Jensen researched the teachings of Jesus out of her very own need to know the Word of our Lord. Then the inevitable happened; she began to teach others what Christ had taught her. It is only after many years of study and application of these truths that those who benefited from them pressed her to publish her research. I'm so glad they did! Christians everywhere will now have a ready reference book that details Christ's instruction on ninety-six topics.

I think you'll be pleasantly surprised at how easy it is to understand the teachings of Jesus as you turn again and again to *Living the Words of Jesus*. Laid out in a very simple manner are His principles, promises, and commands, along with the author's insightful reflections. I expect that many who read this book will learn more than its contents; they will also be challenged to apply these study methods and do their own research on other subjects Christ taught. I know I will.

Now the wrapping paper is off. Open and enjoy this delightful gift and learn what Jesus said.

—Timothy K. Hoke
Faith Presbyterian Church
San Antonio, Texas

# LIVING *the* WORDS *of* JESUS

# INTRODUCTION

*J*esus said, "The words I have spoken to you are spirit and they are life." If we want spiritual life we must have the words of Jesus. Having His words does not mean just knowing what they say from reading them or hearing them read. Having Jesus' words means taking them in by seeing or hearing them, meditating on them to get their meaning, considering how they should apply to us personally, and then putting them into practice. This is the process for making Jesus' words a part of us. Indeed, it is the process for making any part of the Bible our own. It is also the only way to take on the mind of Christ. We cannot know Christ's mind except through His words.

Having the mind of Christ was my goal, so what began as a devotional exercise to become more Christlike in my thinking, developed into a reference book for my personal use. It has become a tool to use when there is ignorance or confusion on a particular subject.

Although I wrote this book originally for my own use, it has been used by many other people. It has been used by parents and teachers in instructing children. My own grandchildren have asked me to include more topics! Men and women who teach adults have also found it helpful. It works well in small groups as a topical study guide for discussion. It will be used in Rafiki Girls' Centers (vocational training centers for teenage girls in developing countries) in teaching English to the many girls who are not able to attend secondary school. The pro-ceeds for the sale of this book will go to fund these Rafiki Girls' Centers.*

The topics are not meant to be read through consecutively, thus the book is laid out as follows for easy reference.

1. The topics are arranged alphabetically.
2. The verses listed as PRINCIPLES give the general meaning Jesus put on the topic.
3. The PROMISES verses help in meditating for personal application.
4. The COMMANDS verses give marching orders straight from the mouth of Jesus.
5. REFLECTIONS are simply a few of my own thoughts.

The book is dedicated to my own three daughters, Annie, Kathy, and Tova, whose lives reflect their own feeding on the words of Jesus. A special thanks goes to Tova for typing the first draft into the computer for me.

I pray that as you use this book in whatever way God leads you, that the words of Jesus will increasingly give you the mind of Christ and bring you that life that only He can give.

—ROSEMARY JENSEN
General Director
The Rafiki Foundation, Inc.

---

*For more information, write The Rafiki Foundation, Inc., 19001 Huebner Road #2, San Antonio, TX 78258; or, www.rafiki-foundation.org.

# A

# ADULTERY

## Principles

Matthew 5:28: Anyone who looks at a woman lustfully has already committed adultery with her in his heart.

Matthew 5:32: Anyone who divorces his wife, except for marital unfaithfulness, causes her to become an adulteress, and anyone who marries the divorced woman commits adultery.

Matthew 15:19: For out of the heart come evil thoughts, murder, adultery, sexual immorality, theft, false testimony, slander.

Matthew 19:9: Anyone who divorces his wife, except for marital unfaithfulness, and marries another woman commits adultery.

Mark 10:12: If [a woman] divorces her husband and marries another man, she commits adultery.

## Promises

John 8:7–11: When they kept on questioning him, he straightened up and said to them, "If any one of you is without sin, let him be the first to throw a stone at her." Again he stooped down and wrote on the ground. At this, those who heard began to go away one at a time, the older ones first, until only Jesus was left, with the woman [who was caught in adultery] still standing there. Jesus straightened up and asked her, "Woman, where are they? Has no one condemned you?" "No one, sir," she said. "Then neither do I condemn you," Jesus declared. "Go now and leave your life of sin."

## Commands

Matthew 19:18: Do not commit adultery.

Mark 10:19: You know the commandments: "Do not . . . commit adultery."

## Reflections

Adultery is sexual unfaithfulness to one's spouse. And, as seen in these verses, divorce and remarriage result in adultery. Jesus stated clearly that adultery is sin and that we are not to engage in it. But Jesus made it clear, too, that adultery is a forgivable sin. Once the sin of adultery has been forgiven, however, it is not to be indulged in again. Therefore, it is important to guard the heart, because out of the heart come the thoughts that lead to the action. In Scripture, the *heart* means the mind and the will.

# ANGER

## *Principles*

Matthew 5:21–22: You have heard that it was said to the people long ago, "Do not murder, and anyone who murders will be subject to judgment." But I tell you that anyone who is angry with his brother will be subject to judgment. . . . But anyone who says, "You fool!" will be in danger of the fire of hell.

Mark 3:5: He looked around at them in anger and, deeply distressed at their stubborn hearts, said to the man, "Stretch out your hand." He stretched it out, and his hand was completely restored.

Mark 10:14: When Jesus saw this, he was indignant. He said to them, "Let the little children come to me, and do not hinder them, for the Kingdom of God belongs to such as these."

John 2:14–17: In the temple courts he found men selling cattle, sheep and doves, and others sitting at tables exchanging money. So he made a whip out of cords, and drove all from the temple area, both sheep and cattle; he scattered the coins of the money changers and overturned their tables. To those who sold doves he said, "Get these out of here! How dare you turn my Father's house into a market!" His disciples remembered that it is written: "Zeal for your house will consume me."

John 3:36: Whoever believes in the Son has eternal life, but whoever rejects the Son will not see life, for God's wrath remains on him.

## Reflections

God is angry with sin, and Jesus repeatedly expressed His anger over sin. I, too, may be angry at sin and over situations that arise as a result of sin, but I am not to be angry with my brother.

How can I be angry with sin and yet not angry with the one who sins? I must realize that anger indicates a desire to destroy. Jesus rebuked people for their sins, but His purpose was never to destroy. Rather, His anger was always redemptive. Redemption, then, is the key. When my anger flares over someone else's sin, do I want to destroy that person or do I want to turn that person from his or her sin? Destructive anger is wrong. Redemptive anger is Christlike.

# APPLICATION

## Principles

Matthew 13:12: Whoever has will be given more, and he will have an abundance. Whoever does not have, even what he has will be taken from him.

Matthew 13:19: When anyone hears the message about the kingdom and does not understand it, the evil one comes and snatches away what was sown in his heart.

Mark 4:24: Consider carefully what you hear. . . . With the measure you use, it will be measured to you—and even more.

Luke 6:47–49: I will show you what he is like who comes to me and hears my words and puts them into practice. He is like a man building a house, who dug down deep and laid the foundation on rock. When a flood came, the torrent struck that house but could not shake it, because it was well built. But the one who hears my words and does not put them into practice is like a man who built a house on the ground without a foundation. The moment the torrent struck that house, it collapsed and its destruction was complete.

## Promises

Luke 8:18: Therefore consider carefully how you listen. Whoever has will be given more; whoever does not have, even what he thinks he has will be taken from him.

Luke 19:26: I tell you that to everyone who has, more will be given, but as for the one who has nothing, even what he has will be taken away.

## Commands

John 5:8: Get up! Pick up your mat and walk.

## Reflections

Use it or lose it. That seems clear from what Jesus says. *It* could refer to many things, but certainly *it* refers to the Word of God.

How often I've read Scripture, not paying attention to what I'm reading and therefore not understanding what God is trying to say to me. At those times, the Devil snatches Scripture away from me.

More often, however, I've read the Scripture, understood it perfectly, but failed to apply it. That's when Scripture is lost—I think I have something but in reality I don't possess it. God, help me to immediately apply those things that You say to me.

# AUTHORITY

## Principles

Matthew 7:28–29: When Jesus had finished saying these things, the crowds were amazed at his teaching, because he taught as one who had authority, and not as their teachers of the law.

Mark 1:34: Jesus healed many who had various diseases. He also drove out many demons, but he would not let the demons speak because they knew who he was.

Mark 4:39–41: He got up, rebuked the wind and said to the waves, "Quiet! Be still!" Then the wind died down and it was completely calm. He said to his disciples, "Why are you so afraid? Do you still have no faith?" They were terrified and asked each other, "Who is this? Even the wind and the waves obey him!"

Luke 18:27: What is impossible with men is possible with God.

John 10:17–18: The reason my Father loves me is that I lay down my life—only to take it up again. No one takes it from me, but I lay it down of my own accord. I have authority to lay it down and authority to take it up again. This command I received from my Father.

John 17:2: For you granted him authority over all people that he might give eternal life to all those you have given him.

## Promises

Matthew 16:19: I will give you the keys of the kingdom of heaven; whatever you bind on earth will be bound in heaven, and whatever you loose on earth will be loosed in heaven.

Matthew 18:18: I tell you the truth, whatever you bind on earth will be bound in heaven, and whatever you loose on earth will be loosed in heaven.

Matthew 28:18: All authority in heaven and on earth has been given to me.

Mark 6:7: Calling the Twelve to him, he sent them out two by two and gave them authority over evil spirits.

Mark 9:23: Everything is possible for him who believes.

John 20:22–23: Receive the Holy Spirit. If you forgive anyone his sins, they are forgiven; if you do not forgive them, they are not forgiven.

## Commands

Matthew 20:25–28: You know that the rulers of the Gentiles lord it over them, and their high officials exercise authority over them. Not so with you. Instead, whoever wants to become great among you must be your servant, and who-ever wants to be first must be your slave—just as the Son of Man did not come to be served, but to serve, and to give his life as a ransom for many.

Luke 22:25–27: The kings of the Gentiles lord it over them; and those who exercise authority over them call themselves Benefactors. But you are not to be like that. Instead, the greatest among you should be like the youngest, and the one who rules like the one who serves. For who is greater, the one who is at the table or the one who serves? Is it not the one who is at the table? But I am among you as one who serves.

## Reflections

*Authority* is the right to exercise power over others. We do not have inherent authority; it must be given to us by another. Thus, assuming authority that has not been given is presumption. Any authority we have as Christian leaders must be given to us by the Lord. The authority that Jesus gives will manifest itself in servanthood.

---
B
---

# BAPTISM

## Principles

Mark 16:16: Whoever believes and is baptized will be saved, but whoever does not believe will be condemned.

John 3:5: I tell you the truth, no one can enter the Kingdom of God unless he is born of water and the Spirit.

Acts 1:4–5: Do not leave Jerusalem, but wait for the gift my Father promised, which you have heard me speak about. For John baptized with water, but in a few days you will be baptized with the Holy Spirit.

## Promises

Acts 1:7–8: It is not for you to know the times or dates the Father has set by his own authority. But you will receive power when the Holy Spirit comes on you; and you will be my witnesses in Jerusalem, and in all Judea and Samaria, and to the ends of the earth.

## Commands

Matthew 28:19–20: Therefore go and make disciples of all nations, baptizing them in the name of the Father and of the Son and of the Holy Spirit, and teaching them to obey everything I have commanded you. And surely I am with you always, to the very end of the age.

## Reflections

Baptism is the sacrament of initiation. Jesus was baptized—not for repentance, but to identify with humanity and to initiate His earthly ministry. All those who want to be initiated into the Kingdom of God must be baptized with the Holy Spirit. At the time of belief in the Lord Jesus Christ, Christians receive the baptism of the Holy Spirit, which initiates life with Christ. Baptism by water—which may occur before or after the baptism of the Holy Spirit—for the remission of sins is the outward sign of the inward work of the Holy Spirit. Therefore, I am commanded to go to all nations and baptize them. But the baptism must be accompanied by discipling and by teaching obedience to God.

# BLASPHEMY

## Principles

Matthew 12:31–32: Every sin and blasphemy will be forgiven men, but the blasphemy against the Spirit will not be forgiven. Anyone who speaks a word against the Son of Man will be forgiven, but anyone who speaks against the Holy Spirit will not be forgiven, either in this age or in the age to come.

Mark 3:29: But whoever blasphemes against the Holy Spirit will never be forgiven; he is guilty of an eternal sin.

Luke 12:10: And everyone who speaks a word against the Son of Man will be forgiven, but anyone who blasphemes against the Holy Spirit will not be forgiven.

## Reflections

*Blasphemy* means bringing reproach against God. These verses state that all blasphemies will be forgiven—except blasphemy against the Holy Spirit. The verses use the present tense, indicating that only continuous blasphemy against the Holy Spirit will not be forgiven. Past blasphemies, of which one repents, are not necessarily included here.

# BLESSING

## Principles

Luke 10:23–24: Blessed are the eyes that see what you see. For I tell you that many prophets and kings wanted to see what you see but did not see it, and to hear what you hear but did not hear it.

Luke 11:28: Blessed rather are those who hear the word of God and obey it.

## Promises

Matthew 5:3–12: Blessed are the poor in spirit, for theirs is the kingdom of heaven. Blessed are those who mourn, for they will be comforted. Blessed are the meek, for they will inherit the earth. Blessed are those who hunger and thirst for righteousness, for they will be filled. Blessed are the merciful, for they will be shown mercy. Blessed are the pure in heart, for they will see God. Blessed are the peacemakers, for they will be called sons of God. Blessed are those who are persecuted because of righteousness, for theirs is the kingdom of heaven. Blessed are you when people insult you, persecute you and falsely say all kinds of evil against you because of me. Rejoice and be glad, because great is your reward in heaven, for in the same way they persecuted the prophets who were before you.

Luke 6:20–23: Blessed are you who are poor, for yours is the Kingdom of God. Blessed are you who hunger now, for you will be satisfied. Blessed are you who weep now, for you will laugh. Blessed are you when men hate you, when they exclude you and insult you and reject your name as evil, because of the Son of Man. Rejoice in that day and leap for joy, because great is your reward in heaven. For that is how their fathers treated the prophets.

Luke 7:23: Blessed is the man who does not fall away on account of me.

## Reflections

There are no commands to be blessed, since blessing is something we receive. We look for God's blessing in good things, but His blessings often come through what we humanly perceive as troubles. Yet we can experience great joy in the midst of suffering—if we are suffering in the will of God. Jesus wants to encourage and comfort in time of suffering. He loves me and wants me to know there's a reason for, and an end to, my troubles. His presence is the greatest of all blessings, and that blessing, of course, always accompanies obedience to God's Word.

# C

# CHILDREN

## *Principles*

Matthew 10:37: Anyone who loves his son or daughter more than me is not worthy of me.

Matthew 18:6: If anyone causes one of these little ones who believe in me to sin, it would be better for him to have a large millstone hung around his neck and to be drowned in the depths of the sea.

Luke 14:26: If anyone comes to me and does not hate his father and mother, his wife and children, his brothers and sisters—yes, even his own life—he cannot be my disciple.

Luke 18:17: Anyone who will not receive the Kingdom of God like a little child will never enter it.

## *Promises*

Matthew 18:1–4: The disciples came to Jesus and asked, "Who is the greatest in the kingdom of heaven?" He called a little child and had him stand among them. And he said: "I tell you the truth, unless you change and become like little children, you will never enter the kingdom of heaven. Therefore, whoever humbles himself like this child is the greatest in the kingdom of heaven.

Mark 9:37: Whoever welcomes one of these little children in my name welcomes me.

Luke 8:49–56: While Jesus was still speaking, someone came from the house of Jairus, the synagogue ruler. "Your daughter is dead," he said. "Don't bother the teacher any more." Hearing this, Jesus said to Jairus, "Don't be afraid; just believe, and she will be healed." When he arrived at the house of Jairus, he did not let anyone go in with him except Peter, John and James, and the child's father and mother. Meanwhile, all the people were wailing and mourning for her. "Stop wailing," Jesus said. "She is not dead but asleep." They laughed at him, knowing that she was dead. But he took her by the hand and said, "My child, get up!" Her spirit returned, and at once she stood up. Then Jesus told them to give her something to eat. Her parents were astonished, but he ordered them not to tell anyone what had happened.

Luke 9:46–48: An argument started among the disciples as to which of them would be the greatest. Jesus, knowing their thoughts, took a little child and had him stand beside him. Then he said to them, "Whoever welcomes this little child in my name welcomes me; and whoever welcomes me welcomes the one who sent me. For he who is least among you all—he is the greatest."

## Commands

Matthew 18:10: See that you do not look down on one of these little ones. For I tell you that their angels in heaven always see the face of my Father in heaven.

Matthew 19:13–14: Then little children were brought to Jesus for him to place his hands on them and pray for them. But the disciples rebuked those who brought them. Jesus said, "Let the little children come to me, and do not hinder them, for the kingdom of heaven belongs to such as these."

## Reflections

God cares for children, and He tells me that I am not to look down upon them. Nor am I to hinder them in coming to Christ. It would be better, in fact, if I had never lived than to cause a child of God to sin. I must, therefore, be very careful how I walk before children, how I advise them, and how I relate to them. A careful walk is especially necessary before my own children and grandchildren, over whom I have the most influence. I am encouraged, though, in Jesus' promise that whatever I do for children in His name, I do for Him. What a great incentive for working with children!

Beyond that, I am to become like a child in faith, my trust in God being simple and complete. Jesus loves children. During His earthly ministry, He wanted them around, He hugged them and touched them to bless them. He protected them and wanted them to receive an inheritance.

# CHURCH

## Principles

Matthew 18:15–17: If your brother sins against you, go and show him his fault, just between the two of you. If he listens to you, you have won your brother over. But if he will not listen, take one or two others along, so that "every matter may be established by the testimony of two or three witnesses." If he refuses to listen to them, tell it to the church; and if he refuses to listen even to the church, treat him as you would a pagan or a tax collector.

John 10:16: I have other sheep that are not of this sheep pen. I must bring them also. They too will listen to my voice, and there shall be one flock and one shepherd.

John 17:20–23: I pray . . . that all of them may be one, Father, just as you are in me and I am in you. May they also be in us so that the world may believe that you have sent me. I have given them the glory that you gave me, that they may be one as we are one: I in them and you in me. May they be brought to complete unity to let the world know that you sent me and have loved them even as you have loved me.

## Promises

Matthew 16:18: And I tell you that you are Peter, and on this rock I will build my church, and the gates of Hades will not overcome it.

## Reflections

The church consists of God's called-out people. They are from every land and are of every color. It's exciting when we travel throughout the world and find other called-out people. Ground rules have been laid out, however, for living with other Christians. Jesus desires that we live together in unity.

Jesus promises that those in His church will not be overcome by death. They may die physically, but they will receive new spiritual bodies and will live eternally with Christ.

# CLEANNESS

## Principles

Matthew 23:27–28: Woe to you, teachers of the law and Pharisees, you hypocrites! You are like whitewashed tombs, which look beautiful on the outside but on the inside are full of dead men's bones and everything unclean. In the same way, on the outside you appear to people as righteous but on the inside you are full of hypocrisy and wickedness.

Mark 7:18–23: "Are you so dull?" he asked. "Don't you see that nothing that enters a man from the outside can make him 'unclean'? For it doesn't go into his heart but into his stomach, and then out of his body." (In saying this, Jesus declared all foods "clean.") He went on: "What comes out of a man is what makes him 'unclean.' For from within, out of men's hearts, come evil thoughts, sexual immorality, theft, murder, adultery, greed, malice, deceit, lewdness, envy, slander, arrogance and folly. All these evils come from inside and make a man 'unclean.'"

John 13:10: A person who has had a bath needs only to wash his feet; his whole body is clean.

## Promises

Luke 11:39–41: Now then, you Pharisees clean the outside of the cup and dish, but inside you are full of greed and wickedness. You foolish people! Did not the one who made the outside make the inside also? But give what is inside the dish to the poor, and everything will be clean for you.

## Commands

Matthew 23:25–26: Woe to you, teachers of the law and Pharisees, you hypocrites! You clean the outside of the cup and dish, but inside they are full of greed and self-indulgence. Blind Pharisee! First clean the inside of the cup and dish, and then the outside also will be clean.

## Reflections

Jesus is clean. He is holy.

My cleanness of life doesn't come from the outside but from the inside. Once my life has been cleansed by the Lord Jesus Christ, I need only take care of the things that dirty me as they occur. But I am told to take care of those things daily. It is deadly to dwell upon sins once they have been forgiven; doing so renders me powerless for all that God wants me to do.

On the other hand, I must remember an important principle: The evil within me will exist until I am made incorruptible. I am clean in Christ Jesus, but my body will be made permanently clean only when Christ changes it. Thus, the corruption that is within me must be addressed immediately, as soon as the Holy Spirit brings something to my consciousness. I must confess it quickly before it first defiles me and then those around me.

The potential for corruption is always present in this life, but I can be cleansed of corruption when, as soon as I'm convicted of it, I take it to Christ.

# COMFORT

## Promises

Matthew 5:4: Blessed are those who mourn, for they will be comforted.

John 14:16: I will ask the Father, and he will give you another Counselor to be with you forever.

John 14:26: The Counselor, the Holy Spirit, whom the Father will send in my name, will teach you all things and will remind you of everything I have said to you.

John 14:27: Peace I leave with you; my peace I give you. I do not give to you as the world gives. Do not let your hearts be troubled and do not be afraid.

John 15:5: I am the vine; you are the branches. If a man remains in me and I in him, he will bear much fruit; apart from me you can do nothing.

John 15:7: If you remain in me and my words remain in you, ask whatever you wish, and it will be given you.

John 16:33: I have told you these things, so that in me you may have peace. In this world you will have trouble. But take heart! I have overcome the world.

## Reflections

*Comfort* is the presence of consolation and strength in a time of need. I will find consolation and strength, for instance, when I mourn over my sins. I also receive unmerited comfort from the grace of God when I'm in the midst of troubles, troubles that I'm bound to experience in this world. Jesus gives peace that comforts me; it consists of knowing that He is present, and that He is in control of my circumstances. He is the Comforter, and I am connected to Him.

---
D
---

# DISCERNMENT

## Principles

Matthew 7:18: A good tree cannot bear bad fruit, and a bad tree cannot bear good fruit.

Matthew 7:20: By their fruit you will recognize them.

Matthew 22:29: You are in error because you do not know the Scriptures or the power of God.

Mark 13:28: Learn this lesson from the fig tree: As soon as its twigs get tender and its leaves come out, you know that summer is near.

Luke 11:34: Your eye is the lamp of your body. When your eyes are good, your whole body also is full of light. But when they are bad, your body also is full of darkness.

## Promises

Luke 11:36: Therefore, if your whole body is full of light, and no part of it dark, it will be completely lighted, as when the light of a lamp shines on you.

## Commands

Matthew 7:6: Do not give dogs what is sacred; do not throw your pearls to pigs. If you do, they may trample them under their feet, and then turn and tear you to pieces.

Matthew 7:13–14: Enter through the narrow gate. For wide is the gate and broad is the road that leads to destruction, and many enter through it. But small is the gate and narrow the road that leads to life, and only a few find it.

Matthew 23:3: You must obey [the teachers of the Law and the Pharisees] and do everything they tell you. But do not do what they do, for they do not practice what they preach.

Matthew 24:6: You will hear of wars and rumors of wars, but see to it that you are not alarmed. Such things must happen, but the end is still to come.

Matthew 24:24–26: False Christs and false prophets will appear and perform great signs and miracles to deceive even the elect—if that were possible. See, I have told you ahead of time. So if anyone tells you, "There he is, out in the desert," do not go out; or, "Here he is, in the inner rooms," do not believe it.

Luke 11:35: See to it, then, that the light within you is not darkness.

## Reflections

Jesus was discerning, able to discern the right time to act, discerning of people, knowing those who were genuine and those who were not. He knew what to do and say because He did and said only that which His Father told Him.

*The words of Jesus on discernment are mostly warnings:*
1. Don't share the Lord's work with unbelievers, and don't try to advise those who are not willing to change. They only turn on you.
2. Stay narrow-minded when it comes to things of the Lord.
3. Serve those in authority over you, but don't become like them if they are not genuine.
4. Don't be alarmed in regard to what you hear about world conditions. Listen to what the Lord says about the events of the world.
5. Take care that the principles you live by are not false principles.

*Several good principles to follow:*
1. To discern between people who are led of the Lord and those who are not, look at the results of their lives. What actions do you see? How are others affected by their lives? What character traits are evident?
2. Knowing the Scriptures gives you the basis for discernment.
3. Keep your eyes open and keep them pure.
4. Each day, draw on the life of Christ within for the discernment you need.

# DISCIPLESHIP

## *Principles*

Matthew 8:19–22: A teacher of the law came to him and said, "Teacher, I will follow you wherever you go." Jesus replied, "Foxes have holes and birds of the air have nests, but the Son of Man has no place to lay his head." Another disciple said to him, "Lord, first let me go and bury my father." But Jesus told him, "Follow me, and let the dead bury their own dead."

Matthew 10:38: Anyone who does not take his cross and follow me is not worthy of me.

Matthew 12:49–50: Pointing to his disciples, he said, "Here are my mother and my brothers. For whoever does the will of my Father in heaven is my brother and sister and mother."

Matthew 16:25: Whoever wants to save his life will lose it, but whoever loses his life for me will find it.

Mark 10:43–44: Whoever wants to become great among you must be your servant, and whoever wants to be first must be slave of all.

Luke 6:40: A student is not above his teacher, but everyone who is fully trained will be like his teacher.

Luke 9:23: If anyone would come after me, he must deny himself and take up his cross daily and follow me.

Luke 9:62: No one who puts his hand to the plow and looks back is fit for service in the Kingdom of God.

Luke 14:26–27: If anyone comes to me and does not hate his father and mother, his wife and children, his brothers and sisters—yes, even his own life—he cannot be my disciple. And anyone who does not carry his cross and follow me cannot be my disciple.

Luke 14:33: Any of you who does not give up everything he has cannot be my disciple.

John 10:27: My sheep listen to my voice; I know them, and they follow me.

John 12:26: Whoever serves me must follow me; and where I am, my servant also will be. My Father will honor the one who serves me.

John 15:20–21: Remember the words I spoke to you: "No servant is greater than his master." If they persecuted me, they will persecute you also. If they obeyed my teaching, they will obey yours also. They will treat you this way because of my name, for they do not know the One who sent me.

## Promises

Matthew 4:19: Come, follow me, . . . and I will make you fishers of men.

Matthew 11:29: Take my yoke upon you and learn from me, for I am gentle and humble in heart, and you will find rest for your souls.

Mark 10:29–30: No one who has left home or brothers or sisters or mother or father or children or fields for me and the gospel will fail to receive a hundred times as much in this present age (homes, brothers, sisters, mothers, children and fields—and with them, persecutions) and in the age to come, eternal life.

John 8:31–32: If you hold to my teaching, you are really my disciples. Then you will know the truth, and the truth will set you free.

John 15:8: This is to my Father's glory, that you bear much fruit, showing yourselves to be my disciples.

John 15:16: You did not choose me, but I chose you and appointed you to go and bear fruit—fruit that will last. Then the Father will give you whatever you ask in my name.

## Commands

Matthew 28:19: Go and make disciples of all nations, baptizing them in the name of the Father and of the Son and of the Holy Spirit.

Mark 1:17–18: Come, follow me, . . . and I will make you fishers of men.

John 13:34–35: A new command I give you: Love one another. As I have loved you, so you must love one another.

By this all men will know that you are my disciples, if you love one another.

John 21:22: What is that to you? You must follow me.

## Reflections

Jesus is the perfect leader, the master teacher. And discipleship means following the lifestyle outlined by Jesus. Being a disciple of Jesus will give me rest for my soul and make me a fisher of people, but the way will never be easy. I have to deny myself, and denying myself means ignoring myself, something that doesn't come naturally. Rather, denying self takes daily discipline, starting each day by giving everything to Jesus, surrendering every aspect of my life to Him, and making myself available for His use—no matter what it is.

Discipleship involves, too, taking up a cross—a voluntary act that in some way brings life to others. It involves suffering that I deliberately take on—not in a masochistic way but in joy, knowing that it is the Father's will for me and that it gives something to another person.

Following Jesus, denying self, taking up the cross—none of this can be done without the empowering of the Holy Spirit.

# DISCRETION

## Principles

Matthew 10:16: I am sending you out like sheep among wolves. Therefore be as shrewd as snakes and as innocent as doves.

Matthew 24:28: Wherever there is a carcass, there the vultures will gather.

Matthew 26:52: All who draw the sword will die by the sword.

Luke 16:8–9: The master commended the dishonest manager because he had acted shrewdly. For the people of this world are more shrewd in dealing with their own kind than are the people of the light. I tell you, use worldly wealth to gain friends for yourselves, so that when it is gone, you will be welcomed into eternal dwellings.

## Commands

Matthew 4:7: Do not put the Lord your God to the test.

Matthew 7:6: Do not give dogs what is sacred; do not throw your pearls to pigs. If you do, they may trample them under their feet, and then turn and tear you to pieces.

Matthew 10:17: Be on your guard against men.

Matthew 22:21: Give to Caesar what is Caesar's, and to God what is God's.

John 6:12: When they had all had enough to eat, he said to his disciples, "Gather the pieces that are left over. Let nothing be wasted."

## Reflections

A long time ago I asked the Lord to speak to me each morning. He does—when I listen. Here are some things He has said to me.

Don't be stupid in the way you live. I've given you the gift of judgment—use it. You'll encounter both dogs (unbelievers) and pigs (those who take from you and then criticize you for what you give them), so use your head—don't try to share with unbelievers the things I've given you. They can't understand, and they'll think you're a religious fanatic. Don't try to teach self-centered people the precious things I've taught you. They don't want to change; they want only to take what you have and either claim it as their own or use your words against you for their own benefit.

You are sent into the world by Me and it won't be easy.

Not all people are Christian and even Christians do not behave always in a Christlike manner. Sometimes they're influenced by the Devil and can hurt you if you're not careful. So use your head—stay out of trouble and don't make Me have to bail you out. Avoid unnecessary battles, because if you start a fight, you'll likely be injured.

Give the world its due but give also to God that which is due to Him—namely your life.

I will give you all you need—spiritual support as well as

physical provision—but don't waste it. Everything I give is useful, so don't throw it away.

Jesus always knows the right thing to do and the right time to do it.

# DIVISION

## Principles

Mark 3:25: If a house is divided against itself, that house cannot stand.

Luke 11:17: Any kingdom divided against itself will be ruined, and a house divided against itself will fall.

Luke 12:51–53: Do you think I came to bring peace on earth? No, I tell you, but division. From now on there will be five in one family divided against each other, three against two and two against three. They will be divided, father against son and son against father, mother against daughter and daughter against mother, mother-in-law against daughter-in-law and daughter-in-law against mother-in-law.

## Reflections

God sometimes divides Christians from nonbelievers, but we are never to be divided among ourselves. A divided house cannot stand.

In the same way, if I want to accomplish anything, I must strive to obtain personal unity with Christ—in my work, in my home, and most of all in myself. If I'm double-minded—trying to serve both Christ and myself—I will fall; if I hate myself, I will fall; if I'm confused or if I'm frustrated over my failures, I will fall. But Jesus becomes integrated with my inner self, thus giving me peace.

How is this integration accomplished? Through the indwelling of the Holy Spirit and through my knowing the mind of Christ. My body, for example, is neutral; it always does what my mind tells it to do. If, over time, my mind repeatedly tells my body to do something, it will act without conscious thought, as in driving a car. But when the Holy Spirit comes to indwell me, I want Him to control my mind. So I must make a conscious choice to put my mind under the control of the Holy Spirit. Knowing the mind of Christ is my goal, so that as I trust the Holy Spirit to control, He draws on what I have learned of Christ's mind. When my mind, through the Holy Spirit, is integrated with the mind of Christ, I have peace.

# DIVORCE

## Principles

Matthew 5:32–33: Anyone who divorces his wife, except for marital unfaithfulness, causes her to become an adulteress, and anyone who marries the divorced woman commits adultery.

Matthew 19:8–9: Moses permitted you to divorce your wives because your hearts were hard. But it was not this way from the beginning. I tell you that anyone who divorces his wife, except for marital unfaithfulness, and marries another woman commits adultery.

Mark 10:5–9: It was because your hearts were hard that Moses wrote you this law [concerning a certificate of divorce]. . . . But at the beginning of creation God "made them male and female." "For this reason a man will leave his father and mother and be united to his wife, and the two will become one flesh." So they are no longer two, but one. Therefore what God has joined together, let man not separate.

Mark 10:11–12: Anyone who divorces his wife and marries another woman commits adultery against her. And if she divorces her husband and marries another man, she commits adultery.

Luke 16:18: Anyone who divorces his wife and marries another woman commits adultery, and the man who marries a divorced woman commits adultery.

## Promises

John 4:17–19: "I have no husband," she replied. Jesus said to her, "You are right when you say you have no husband. The fact is, you have had five husbands, and the man you now have is not your husband. What you have just said is quite true." "Sir," the woman said, "I can see that you are a prophet."

John 4:29: Come, see a man who told me everything I ever did. Could this be the Christ?

John 4:39: Many of the Samaritans from that town believed in him because of the woman's testimony, "He told me everything I ever did.'

## Commands

Mark 10:9: What God has joined together, let man not separate.

## Reflections

Divorce is the breaking of the marital bond. There is more than one way of separating two people who have been joined together by God, but the marital bond is broken only by divorce or death.

Divorce was not part of God's original plan at the Creation. Rather, divorce is the result of human stubbornness. According to Jesus, marriage is binding and divorce is permitted only in instances of adultery. Nonetheless, Jesus is forgiving, and divorce is a pardonable sin. The Samaritan woman confessed her sin, believed Jesus, was saved, and all her previous life was washed away.

# ELECTION

## Principles

Matthew 22:14: Many are invited, but few are chosen.

John 10:2–5: The man who enters by the gate is the shepherd of his sheep. The watchman opens the gate for him, and the sheep listen to his voice. He calls his own sheep by name and leads them out. When he has brought out all his own, he goes on ahead of them, and his sheep follow him because they know his voice. But they will never follow a stranger; in fact, they will run away from him because they do not recognize a stranger's voice.

## Promises

John 15:16: You did not choose me, but I chose you and appointed you to go and bear fruit—fruit that will last. Then the Father will give you whatever you ask in my name.

## Reflections

*Election* means to be chosen by God. He, not the sinner, does the choosing. *Jesus wants me* is a concept so amazing, it is scarcely to be believed. And not only does He want me, but He cares for me, provides for me, and protects me. He chose me to bear eternal fruit, and He promises to answer my prayers. What could be more wonderful than that?

# ENEMIES

## Principles

Matthew 5:39–42: Do not resist an evil person. If someone strikes you on the right cheek, turn to him the other also. If someone wants to sue you and take your tunic, let him have your cloak as well. If someone forces you to go one mile, go with him two miles. Give to the one who asks you, and do not turn away from the one who wants to borrow from you.

Matthew 5:44–45: Love your enemies and pray for those who persecute you, that you may be sons of your Father in heaven. He causes his sun to rise on the evil and the good, and sends rain on the righteous and the unrighteous.

Luke 23:34: Jesus said, "Father, forgive them, for they do not know what they are doing." And they divided up his clothes by casting lots.

## Promises

Luke 6:35: Love your enemies, do good to them, and lend to them without expecting to get anything back. Then your reward will be great, and you will be sons of the Most High, because he is kind to the ungrateful and wicked.

## Commands

Luke 6:27–28: Love your enemies, do good to those who hate you, bless those who curse you, pray for those who mistreat you.

## Reflections

To love my enemies, I must ask the Holy Spirit to help me. I can't control my emotions, but I can, with the Spirit's help, control my actions. That's why I am commanded to "do good to," "bless," and "pray for" those who hate me, curse me, or mistreat me.

The process for loving others goes something like this: As I commit my body to obey what God commands, my heart begins to love God more and more. As my heart grows in love toward God, it gradually takes on His character, identifying itself as His child and thus growing godlike. Out of a godlike heart will come love for others—including my enemies.

Jesus serves as the perfect example. Even as the soldiers nailed Him to the cross, He asked His Father to forgive them. Because He loved them, He attributed the best interpretation possible to their motives: "They do not know what they are doing."

# ETERNAL LIFE

## *Principles*

Matthew 18:14: Your Father in heaven is not willing that any of these little ones should be lost.

Matthew 25:46: [Some] will go away to eternal punishment, but the righteous to eternal life.

Mark 2:17: It is not the healthy who need a doctor, but the sick. I have not come to call the righteous, but sinners.

Mark 10:23: How hard it is for the rich to enter the Kingdom of God!

Mark 10:25: It is easier for a camel to go through the eye of a needle than for a rich man to enter the Kingdom of God.

Mark 16:16: Whoever believes and is baptized will be saved, but whoever does not believe will be condemned.

Luke 18:17: Anyone who will not receive the Kingdom of God like a little child will never enter it.

Luke 19:10: The Son of Man came to seek and to save what was lost.

John 3:3: No one can see the Kingdom of God unless he is born again.

John 3:5–8: No one can enter the Kingdom of God unless he is born of water and the Spirit. Flesh gives birth to flesh, but the Spirit gives birth to spirit. You should not be surprised at my saying, "You must be born again." The wind blows wherever it pleases. You hear its sound, but you cannot tell where it comes from or where it is going. So it is with everyone born of the Spirit.

John 3:36: Whoever believes in the Son has eternal life, but whoever rejects the Son will not see life, for God's wrath remains on him.

John 6:44–45: No one can come to me unless the Father who sent me draws him, and I will raise him up at the last day. It is written in the Prophets: "They will all be taught by God." Everyone who listens to the Father and learns from him comes to me.

John 8:24: I told you that you would die in your sins; if you do not believe that I am the one I claim to be, you will indeed die in your sins.

John 13:20: Whoever accepts anyone I send accepts me; and whoever accepts me accepts the one who sent me.

John 17:3: This is eternal life: that they may know you, the only true God, and Jesus Christ, whom you have sent.

## Promises

John 3:16–18: God so loved the world that he gave his one and only Son, that whoever believes in him shall not perish but have eternal life. For God did not send his Son into the world to condemn the world, but to save the world through him. Whoever believes in him is not condemned, but whoever does not believe stands condemned already because he has not believed in the name of God's one and only Son.

John 4:13–14: Everyone who drinks this water will be thirsty again, but whoever drinks the water I give him will never thirst. Indeed, the water I give him will become in him a spring of water welling up to eternal life.

John 5:24: Whoever hears my word and believes him who sent me has eternal life and will not be condemned; he has crossed over from death to life.

John 6:39–40: This is the will of him who sent me, that I shall lose none of all that he has given me, but raise them up at the last day. For my Father's will is that everyone who looks to the Son and believes in him shall have eternal life, and I will raise him up at the last day.

John 6:47: He who believes has everlasting life.

John 6:51: I am the living bread that came down from heaven. If anyone eats of this bread, he will live forever. This bread is my flesh, which I will give for the life of the world.

John 6:54: Whoever eats my flesh and drinks my blood has eternal life, and I will raise him up at the last day.

John 6:58: This is the bread that came down from heaven. Your forefathers ate manna and died, but he who feeds on this bread will live forever.

John 8:51: If anyone keeps my word, he will never see death.

John 10:9–10: I am the gate; whoever enters through me will be saved. He will come in and go out, and find pasture. The thief comes only to steal and kill and destroy; I have come that they may have life, and have it to the full.

John 10:28–29: I give them eternal life, and they shall never perish; no one can snatch them out of my hand. My Father, who has given them to me, is greater than all; no one can snatch them out of my Father's hand.

John 11:25–26: I am the resurrection and the life. He who believes in me will live, even though he dies; and whoever lives and believes in me will never die.

John 12:25: The man who loves his life will lose it, while the man who hates his life in this world will keep it for eternal life.

## Commands

Luke 10:20: Do not rejoice that the spirits submit to you, but rejoice that your names are written in heaven.

Luke 13:24: Make every effort to enter through the narrow door, because many, I tell you, will try to enter and will not be able to.

John 6:27: Do not work for food that spoils, but for food that endures to eternal life, which the Son of Man will give you. On him God the Father has placed his seal of approval.

## Reflections

*Eternal* means without end in time. Jesus had much to say about eternal life, commanding that we make every effort to enter into it. He leaves no doubt that He came to give it and that He wants every person to believe it. And He makes many promises that whoever believes in Him will have it. He promises, too, that eternal life is not just a blissful state after death, but means that those who believe on Him will have an immediate fullness and quality of life.

# EVIL

## Principles

Matthew 5:11: Blessed are you when people insult you, persecute you and falsely say all kinds of evil against you because of me.

Matthew 5:45: He causes his sun to rise on the evil and the good, and sends rain on the righteous and the unrighteous.

Matthew 6:13: Lead us not into temptation, but deliver us from the evil one.

Matthew 7:11: If you, then, though you are evil, know how to give good gifts to your children, how much more will your Father in heaven give good gifts to those who ask him!

Matthew 9:4: Why do you entertain evil thoughts in your hearts?

Matthew 12:34–35: You brood of vipers, how can you who are evil say anything good? For out of the overflow of the heart the mouth speaks. The good man brings good things out of the good stored up in him, and the evil man brings evil things out of the evil stored up in him.

Matthew 13:19: When anyone hears the message about the kingdom and does not understand it, the evil one comes and snatches away what was sown in his heart.

Matthew 13:38: The field is the world, and the good seed stands for the sons of the kingdom. The weeds are the sons of the evil one.

Matthew 13:41: The Son of Man will send out his angels, and they will weed out of his kingdom everything that causes sin and all who do evil.

Matthew 15:19: Out of the heart come evil thoughts, murder, adultery, sexual immorality, theft, false testimony, slander.

Luke 6:9: Which is lawful on the Sabbath: to do good or to do evil, to save life or to destroy it?

Luke 6:22: Blessed are you when men hate you, when they exclude you and insult you and reject your name as evil, because of the Son of Man.

Luke 6:45: The good man brings good things out of the good stored up in his heart, and the evil man brings evil things out of the evil stored up in his heart. For out of the overflow of his heart his mouth speaks.

Luke 11:13: If you then, though you are evil, know how to give good gifts to your children, how much more will your Father in heaven give the Holy Spirit to those who ask him!

Luke 11:24: When an evil spirit comes out of a man, it goes through arid places seeking rest and does not find it. Then it says, "I will return to the house I left."

John 3:19–20: This is the verdict: Light has come into the world, but men loved darkness instead of light because their deeds were evil. Everyone who does evil hates the light, and will not come into the light for fear that his deeds will be exposed.

John 5:29: Those who have done good will rise to live, and those who have done evil will rise to be condemned.

John 7:7: The world cannot hate you, but it hates me because I testify that what it does is evil.

John 17:15: My prayer is not that you take them out of the world but that you protect them from the evil one.

## Commands

Matthew 5:37: Simply let your "Yes" be "Yes," and your "No," "No"; anything beyond this comes from the evil one.

Matthew 5:39: Do not resist an evil person. If someone strikes you on the right cheek, turn to him the other also.

## Reflections

One thing is clear—Jesus has power over the evil in the world. He spoke often of evil and faced it head on, identifying Himself as the One against evil and stating that those who follow Him will also experience evil. He explained, too, that evil thoughts come from an evil heart, and that a heart is evil when it belongs to the Evil One. Those who belong to Jesus bring out good things from their hearts, unless the

Devil deceives them. And the Devil can, on occasion, deceive even Christians. But God's good gift of the Holy Spirit keeps a Christian in the truth.

# F

# FAITH

## *Principles*

Matthew 12:39: A wicked and adulterous generation asks for a miraculous sign! But none will be given it except the sign of the prophet Jonah.

Mark 5:34: Daughter, your faith has healed you. Go in peace and be freed from your suffering.

Luke 24:25: How foolish you are, and how slow of heart to believe all that the prophets have spoken!

John 1:12: To all who received him, to those who believed in his name, he gave the right to become children of God.

John 3:12: I have spoken to you of earthly things and you do not believe; how then will you believe if I speak of heavenly things?

John 3:14–17: Just as Moses lifted up the snake in the desert, so the Son of Man must be lifted up, that everyone who believes in him may have eternal life. For God so loved the world that he gave his one and only Son, that whoever believes in him shall not perish but have eternal life. For God did not send his Son into the world to condemn the world, but to save the world through him.

John 5:46–47: If you believed Moses, you would believe me, for he wrote about me. But since you do not believe what he wrote, how are you going to believe what I say?

John 6:29: The work of God is this: to believe in the one he has sent.

John 8:24: I told you that you would die in your sins; if you do not believe that I am . . . , you will indeed die in your sins.

John 12:44–45: When a man believes in me, he does not believe in me only, but in the one who sent me. When he looks at me, he sees the one who sent me.

John 20:29: Because you have seen me, you have believed; blessed are those who have not seen and yet have believed.

John 20:31: But these [miraculous signs] are written that you may believe that Jesus is the Christ, the Son of God, and that by believing you may have life in his name.

## Promises

Matthew 9:29: According to your faith will it be done to you.

Matthew 17:20: If you have faith as small as a mustard seed, you can say to this mountain, "Move from here to there" and it will move. Nothing will be impossible for you.

Matthew 21:21: If you have faith and do not doubt, not only can you do what was done to the fig tree, but also you can say to this mountain, "Go, throw yourself into the sea," and it will be done.

Matthew 25:23: Well done, good and faithful servant! You have been faithful with a few things; I will put you in charge of many things. Come and share your master's happiness!

Mark 9:23: Everything is possible for him who believes.

Mark 11:24: Whatever you ask for in prayer, believe that you have received it, and it will be yours.

John 11:25–26: I am the resurrection and the life. He who believes in me will live, even though he dies; and whoever lives and believes in me will never die. Do you believe this?

John 11:40: Did I not tell you that if you believed, you would see the glory of God?

John 12:46: I have come into the world as a light, so that no one who believes in me should stay in darkness.

John 14:12: Anyone who has faith in me will do what I have been doing. He will do even greater things than these, because I am going to the Father.

John 20:29: Because you have seen me, you have believed; blessed are those who have not seen and yet have believed.

## Commands

Mark 1:15: The Kingdom of God is near. Repent and believe the good news!

Mark 5:36: Don't be afraid; just believe.

Mark 11:22: Have faith in God.

John 12:36: Put your trust in the light while you have it, so that you may become sons of light.

John 14:1: Do not let your hearts be troubled. Trust in God; trust also in me.

John 20:27: Stop doubting and believe.

## Reflections

*Faith* means believing in a person or a teaching. The Christian faith is a belief in the person of the Lord Jesus Christ. He is real—not just something I want to believe because it makes me feel better. Believing in Him, I need not be troubled, because Jesus can be trusted, and I need not fear that I am being deceived by Him. He is God, and He came to love and save me.

When in faith I bring my suffering to Jesus, trusting Him with it, He will free me from its bondage and give me peace. He doesn't always heal my body and take away the pain, but He does remove the emotional suffering involved and give me peace of mind. So I don't need miraculous signs to convince me that Jesus is real, that His peace is authentic, and that His promises are true.

All God wants me to do is believe in Jesus and act accordingly, because believing in Jesus is believing in God. It is essential only, then, that I believe Jesus loves me and wants me to trust Him with every aspect of my life.

# FALSE TEACHERS

## Principles

Matthew 7:15: Watch out for false prophets. They come to you in sheep's clothing, but inwardly they are ferocious wolves.

Matthew 24:5: For many will come in my name, claiming, "I am the Christ," and will deceive many.

Mark 13:22: For false Christs and false prophets will appear and perform signs and miracles to deceive the elect—if that were possible.

John 10:1: I tell you the truth, the man who does not enter the sheep pen by the gate, but climbs in by some other way, is a thief and a robber.

John 10:12–13: The hired hand is not the shepherd who owns the sheep. So when he sees the wolf coming, he abandons the sheep and runs away. Then the wolf attacks the flock and scatters it. The man runs away because he is a hired hand and cares nothing for the sheep.

## Promises

John 10:10: The thief comes only to steal and kill and destroy; I have come that they may have life, and have it to the full.

## Commands

Matthew 15:14: Leave them; they are blind guides. If a blind man leads a blind man, both will fall into a pit.

Matthew 16:6: Be careful. . . . Be on your guard against the yeast of the Pharisees and Sadducees.

Mark 12:38–39: Watch out for the teachers of the law. They like to walk around in flowing robes and be greeted in the marketplaces, and have the most important seats in the synagogues and the places of honor at banquets.

Mark 13:5–6: Watch out that no one deceives you. Many will come in my name, claiming, "I am he," and will deceive many.

## Reflections

Some kinds of education are not beneficial. Some want to educate me in a way that will serve their purposes, but that will bring death to my soul. Their method is to deceive me. They make themselves look attractive and do all they can to persuade me, but their goal is to have power over me. If they find they can't educate me in their ways and control me, then they'll turn on me and attempt to destroy me.

Jesus has warned me to be on guard against false teachers. Not only are they hypocrites, they want me to follow in their false ways. I must reject them and not associate with them because they can be very persuasive. And too much time with them leads me to think as they do.

# FAMILY

## Principles

Matthew 13:57: Only in his hometown and in his own house is a prophet without honor.

Matthew 19:5: A man will leave his father and mother and be united to his wife, and the two will become one flesh.

Luke 14:26: If anyone comes to me and does not hate his father and mother, his wife and children, his brothers and sisters—yes, even his own life—he cannot be my disciple.

## Promises

Matthew 12:50: Whoever does the will of my Father in heaven is my brother and sister and mother.

Mark 10:29–30: No one who has left home or brothers or sisters or mother or father or children or fields for me and the gospel will fail to receive a hundred times as much in this present age (homes, brothers, sisters, mothers, children and fields—and with them, persecutions) and in the age to come, eternal life.

Luke 8:21: My mother and brothers are those who hear God's word and put it into practice.

## Commands

Matthew 8:21–22: Another disciple said to him, "Lord, first let me go and bury my father." But Jesus told him, "Follow me, and let the dead bury their own dead."

## Reflections

God wants us to be in families, and they are to be close units. Family, however, is never to come before Him. Family must be put aside in favor of our relationship with the Lord. When that sacrifice is made, He promises the privilege of discipleship, and that we will enjoy a family relationship with an even greater number of people.

# FEAR

## Principles

Matthew 10:26: Do not be afraid of them. There is nothing concealed that will not be disclosed, or hidden that will not be made known.

Matthew 10:31: Don't be afraid; you are worth more than many sparrows.

Matthew 14:27: Take courage! It is I. Don't be afraid.

Luke 12:32: Do not be afraid, little flock, for your Father has been pleased to give you the kingdom.

## Promises

Luke 8:50: Don't be afraid; just believe, and she will be healed.

John 14:27: Peace I leave with you; my peace I give you. I do not give to you as the world gives. Do not let your hearts be troubled and do not be afraid.

## Commands

Matthew 10:28: Do not be afraid of those who kill the body but cannot kill the soul. Rather, be afraid of the One who can destroy both soul and body in hell.

Mark 5:36: Don't be afraid; just believe.

John 6:20: [Jesus] said to them, "It is I; don't be afraid."

## Reflections

Fear is my apprehension in a threatening situation. But most of my fear centers around what others will think of me if I act in a certain way. It seems that the root cause of fear, then, is pride. Paralyzed by indecision, fearing the disapproval of others, I find myself not acting at all. Thus, fear oppresses me and keeps me from fulfilling my potential.

But Jesus shields His own from what frightens us. He gives us peace in the midst of storm or when the world seems against us. He commands us, in fact, not to fear when He is near.

There is, certainly, a healthy kind of fear, which is really reverence; we are to fear God because we revere Him. He has awful power and can do anything He pleases with us. He can save us or He can throw us into hell. But Jesus promises that when we are part of His flock we have nothing to fear from Him.

# FORGIVENESS

## Principles

Matthew 6:15: If you do not forgive men their sins, your Father will not forgive your sins.

Matthew 18:35: This is how my heavenly Father will treat each of you unless you forgive your brother from your heart.

Luke 7:47: He who has been forgiven little loves little.

Luke 11:4: Forgive us our sins, for we also forgive everyone who sins against us. And lead us not into temptation.

Luke 15:21–24: The son said to him, "Father, I have sinned against heaven and against you. I am no longer worthy to be called your son." But the father said to his servants, "Quick! Bring the best robe and put it on him. Put a ring on his finger and sandals on his feet. Bring the fattened calf and kill it. Let's have a feast and celebrate. For this son of mine was dead and is alive again; he was lost and is found."

Luke 23:34: Jesus said, "Father, forgive them, for they do not know what they are doing."

John 20:23: If you forgive anyone his sins, they are forgiven; if you do not forgive them, they are not forgiven.

## Promises

Matthew 6:14: If you forgive men when they sin against you, your heavenly Father will also forgive you.

Luke 5:20: When Jesus saw their faith, he said, "Friend, your sins are forgiven."

Luke 24:47: Repentance and forgiveness of sins will be preached in his name to all nations, beginning at Jerusalem.

## Commands

Mark 2:5–11: When Jesus saw their faith, he said to the paralytic, "Son, your sins are forgiven." Now some teachers of the law were sitting there, thinking to themselves, "Why does this fellow talk like that? He's blaspheming! Who can forgive sins but God alone?" Immediately Jesus knew in his spirit that this was what they were thinking in their hearts, and he said to them, "Why are you thinking these things? Which is easier: to say to the paralytic, 'Your sins are forgiven,' or to say, 'Get up, take your mat and walk'? But that you may know that the Son of Man has authority on earth to forgive sins . . ." He said to the paralytic, "I tell you, get up, take your mat and go home."

Mark 11:25: When you stand praying, if you hold anything against anyone, forgive him, so that your Father in heaven may forgive you your sins.

Luke 6:37: Do not judge, and you will not be judged. Do not condemn, and you will not be condemned. Forgive, and you will be forgiven.

Luke 17:3–4: Watch yourselves. If your brother sins, rebuke him, and if he repents, forgive him. If he sins against you seven times in a day, and seven times comes back to you and says, "I repent," forgive him.

## Reflections

*Forgiveness* is pardon for human sins and shortcomings. God forgives us, and we are to forgive each other. Yet at times I focus less upon forgiving than upon being forgiven. Jesus emphasizes the reverse; since I have been forgiven, I am never to hold anything against anyone. And that *is* possible. I am to ask myself, "Am I holding anything against anyone? Who?" I am to forgive them—right now. I can forgive in my heart—whether they ask for forgiveness or not—because God has forgiven me.

# FREEDOM

## Principles

John 8:32–34: [Jesus said,]"Then you will know the truth, and the truth will set you free." They answered him, "We are Abraham's descendants and have never been slaves of anyone. How can you say that we shall be set free?" Jesus replied, "I tell you the truth, everyone who sins is a slave to sin."

## Promises

John 8:34–36: Everyone who sins is a slave to sin. Now a slave has no permanent place in the family, but a son belongs to it forever. So if the Son sets you free, you will be free indeed.

## Reflections

*Freedom* is liberation from bondage. Truth liberates, Jesus is the source of truth, and Jesus sets us free indeed. He, as truth and the perfect standard of righteousness, frees us from self-deception and deception by Satan. As God, Jesus frees us from the consequences of sin. Yet Jesus never gives us freedom to do what we want but freedom to do what *He* wants. In this way He liberates us from ourselves and makes it possible for us to reach our full potential in Him.

Sin enslaves us, controls us, dominates us, and dictates our actions. Only Jesus can break sin's power over our lives. This will happen when we:

1. acknowledge our sin;
2. admit that we are powerless to break its hold over us;
3. ask Jesus to free us from it;
4. immediately obey Him in doing everything He tells us to do.

# FRUITFULNESS

## Principles

Luke 6:43: No good tree bears bad fruit, nor does a bad tree bear good fruit.

John 15:1–4: I am the true vine, and my Father is the gardener. He cuts off every branch in me that bears no fruit, while every branch that does bear fruit he prunes so that it will be even more fruitful. You are already clean because of the word I have spoken to you. Remain in me, and I will remain in you. No branch can bear fruit by itself; it must remain in the vine. Neither can you bear fruit unless you remain in me.

John 15:8: This is to my Father's glory, that you bear much fruit, showing yourselves to be my disciples.

John 15:16: You did not choose me, but I chose you and appointed you to go and bear fruit—fruit that will last. Then the Father will give you whatever you ask in my name.

## Promises

John 12:24: I tell you the truth, unless a kernel of wheat falls to the ground and dies, it remains only a single seed. But if it dies, it produces many seeds.

John 15:5: I am the vine; you are the branches. If a man remains in me and I in him, he will bear much fruit; apart from me you can do nothing.

## Reflections

Fruitfulness is not commanded; being fruitful is not a choice but the result of a way of living. Fruitfulness is what comes from being associated with the source—the root—of the tree, which determines the quality of the fruit it bears. The quantity of fruit produced is directly proportionate to the strength of the spirit-life between the source and the branches that bear the fruit.

If anyone wants to bear fruit on his or her own, that person will find himself or herself alone and fruitless. The more that the self-life dies, the more that fruitfulness occurs.

## G

# GIVING

## Principles

Mark 12:43–44: This poor widow has put more into the treasury than all the others. They all gave out of their wealth; but she, out of her poverty, put in everything—all she had to live on.

Luke 6:38: Give, and it will be given to you. A good measure, pressed down, shaken together and running over, will be poured into your lap. For with the measure you use, it will be measured to you.

## Promises

Matthew 6:3–4: When you give to the needy, do not let your left hand know what your right hand is doing, so that your giving may be in secret. Then your Father, who sees what is done in secret, will reward you.

Matthew 10:41–42: Anyone who receives a prophet because he is a prophet will receive a prophet's reward, and anyone who receives a righteous man because he is a righteous man will receive a righteous man's reward. And if anyone gives even a cup of cold water to one of these little ones because he is my disciple, I tell you the truth, he will certainly not lose his reward.

Luke 11:41: Give what is inside the dish to the poor, and everything will be clean for you.

## Commands

Luke 12:33: Sell your possessions and give to the poor. Provide purses for yourselves that will not wear out, a treasure in heaven that will not be exhausted, where no thief comes near and no moth destroys.

Luke 14:12–14: When you give a luncheon or dinner, do not invite your friends, your brothers or relatives, or your rich neighbors; if you do, they may invite you back and so you will be repaid. But when you give a banquet, invite the poor, the crippled, the lame, the blind, and you will be blessed. Although they cannot repay you, you will be repaid at the resurrection of the righteous.

## Reflections

Giving is to be done sacrificially and consistently with no thought of receiving anything in return. When we do things for our relatives and friends, we are really doing these things for ourselves. Birthday and Christmas presents are not real giving because we always expect something in return. True giving means that we expect something only from the Lord—and He will never disappoint us. He will see to it that we receive in the measure that we give.

# GOD'S CARE

## *Principles*

Matthew 6:26: Look at the birds of the air; they do not sow or reap or store away in barns, and yet your heavenly Father feeds them. Are you not much more valuable than they?

Matthew 10:29–31: Are not two sparrows sold for a penny? Yet not one of them will fall to the ground apart from the will of your Father. And even the very hairs of your head are all numbered. So don't be afraid; you are worth more than many sparrows.

Luke 12:27–28: Consider how the lilies grow. They do not labor or spin. Yet I tell you, not even Solomon in all his splendor was dressed like one of these. If that is how God clothes the grass of the field, which is here today, and tomorrow is thrown into the fire, how much more will he clothe you, O you of little faith!

John 10:2–5: The man who enters by the gate is the shepherd of his sheep. The watchman opens the gate for him, and the sheep listen to his voice. He calls his own sheep by name and leads them out. When he has brought out all his own, he goes on ahead of them, and his sheep follow him because they know his voice. But they will never follow a stranger; in fact, they will run away from him because they do not recognize a stranger's voice.

John 10:11: I am the good shepherd. The good shepherd lays down his life for the sheep.

## Promises

Matthew 18:20: Where two or three come together in my name, there am I with them.

Matthew 28:20: Surely I am with you always, to the very end of the age.

John 6:20: He said to them, "It is I; don't be afraid."

John 6:39: This is the will of him who sent me, that I shall lose none of all that he has given me, but raise them up at the last day.

John 10:14–15: I am the good shepherd; I know my sheep and my sheep know me—just as the Father knows me and I know the Father—and I lay down my life for the sheep.

## Commands

Matthew 11:28: Come to me, all you who are weary and burdened, and I will give you rest.

Luke 12:29–32: Do not set your heart on what you will eat or drink; do not worry about it. For the pagan world runs after all such things, and your Father knows that you need them. But seek his kingdom, and these things will be given to you as well. Do not be afraid, little flock, for your Father has been pleased to give you the kingdom.

## Reflections

I don't usually think about God's care for me until I become tired or I'm overloaded, having too much to do and coping with too many problems. Maybe that's why He lets me get tired or troubled—so I'll remember that He is present, offering the rest that I need. God wants me to realize my dependence upon Him. He takes care of me, but He wants me to know it. And it follows, too, that I should give thanks daily for His care.

# GOD'S WILL

## Principles

Matthew 7:21: Not everyone who says to me, "Lord, Lord," will enter the kingdom of heaven, but only he who does the will of my Father who is in heaven.

Matthew 12:50: Whoever does the will of my Father in heaven is my brother and sister and mother.

## Promises

John 7:17: If anyone chooses to do God's will, he will find out whether my teaching comes from God or whether I speak on my own.

John 16:13: But when he, the Spirit of truth, comes, he will guide you into all truth. He will not speak on his own; he will speak only what he hears, and he will tell you what is yet to come.

## Commands

Matthew 6:10: Your kingdom come, your will be done on earth as it is in heaven.

## Reflections

God's will is what God wants us to do. We must choose to do God's will, and the choice is real, even though God is sovereign in His plans for us. Many people call Jesus "Lord," but nonetheless choose not to do God's will, nor do they even want to. The proof of true faith in Christ is in the doing of God's will, and when I do God's will, I am identified with Jesus, who always did the will of the Father. When I choose to obey the Father, the Holy Spirit will guide me into God's will.

# GREATNESS

## Principles

Luke 7:28: I tell you, among those born of women there is no one greater than John; yet the one who is least in the Kingdom of God is greater than he.

Luke 22:25–27: The kings of the Gentiles lord it over them; and those who exercise authority over them call themselves Benefactors. But you are not to be like that. Instead, the greatest among you should be like the youngest, and the one who rules like the one who serves. For who is greater, the one who is at the table or the one who serves? Is it not the one who is at the table? But I am among you as one who serves.

John 13:16: No servant is greater than his master, nor is a messenger greater than the one who sent him.

## Promises

Luke 9:48: Whoever welcomes this little child in my name welcomes me; and whoever welcomes me welcomes the one who sent me. For he who is least among you all—he is the greatest.

## Reflections

There are no commands to become great, because we cannot make ourselves great. Only God can make us great.

From what Jesus says, however, greatness is associated with service. John the Baptist served, good rulers serve, a servant serves, a messenger serves, and those who welcome little children serve. I can't make myself great, but I can make myself serve and leave my stature to the Lord.

# H

# HEART

## Principles

Matthew 11:29: Take my yoke upon you and learn from me, for I am gentle and humble in heart, and you will find rest for your souls.

Matthew 15:18: The things that come out of the mouth come from the heart, and these make a man "unclean."

Mark 2:8: Immediately Jesus knew in his spirit that this was what they were thinking in their hearts, and he said to them, "Why are you thinking these things?"

Mark 7:6: Isaiah was right when he prophesied about you hypocrites; as it is written: "These people honor me with their lips, but their hearts are far from me."

Luke 6:45: The good man brings good things out of the good stored up in his heart, and the evil man brings evil things out of the evil stored up in his heart. For out of the overflow of his heart his mouth speaks.

## Promises

Matthew 5:8: Blessed are the pure in heart, for they will see God.

Mark 11:23: If anyone says to this mountain, "Go, throw yourself into the sea," and does not doubt in his heart but believes that what he says will happen, it will be done for him.

## Commands

Matthew 22:37: Love the Lord your God with all your heart and with all your soul and with all your mind.

## Reflections

The heart is the center of the human being. And Jesus says that from the center of my being I am to love God. When the center of my being is pure, I will see God. But to keep my center pure, my lips must be pure, my love must be pure, my faith and my thoughts must be pure.

Anything that takes over my thought-life in place of Jesus becomes my idol and is like a mountain that impedes my progress. I must, in faith, tell that mountain to throw itself into the sea, where it disappears from view under the surface of the water. It may not be destroyed, but it may remain there, melting down, causing no trouble. As the mountain loses substance, however, substance is added to my heart, reminding me of God's faithfulness in response to my faith.

# HEAVEN

## Principles

Matthew 7:21: Not everyone who says to me, "Lord, Lord," will enter the kingdom of heaven, but only he who does the will of my Father who is in heaven.

Matthew 22:30: At the resurrection people will neither marry nor be given in marriage; they will be like the angels in heaven.

Luke 20:34–36: The people of this age marry and are given in marriage. But those who are considered worthy of taking part in that age and in the resurrection from the dead will neither marry nor be given in marriage, and they can no longer die; for they are like the angels. They are God's children, since they are children of the resurrection.

## Promises

John 14:2–3: In my Father's house are many rooms; if it were not so, I would have told you. I am going there to prepare a place for you. And if I go and prepare a place for you, I will come back and take you to be with me that you also may be where I am.

## Commands

Matthew 6:9: This, then, is how you should pray: "Our Father in heaven, hallowed be your name."

Matthew 6:20: But store up for yourselves treasures in heaven, where moth and rust do not destroy, and where thieves do not break in and steal.

Luke 10:20: Do not rejoice that the spirits submit to you, but rejoice that your names are written in heaven.

## Reflections

Heaven is the eternal dwelling place of the Father, the place from where Jesus descended and from where the Holy Spirit is received. Heaven is a place, and Jesus contrasts it with earth. Earth, he said, is insecure and fleeting and will pass away, but heaven is permanent and eternal. Heaven was Jesus' home, to which He returned to prepare a place for me and His other children.

# HOLY SPIRIT

## *Principles*

Mark 3:29: Whoever blasphemes against the Holy Spirit will never be forgiven; he is guilty of an eternal sin.

Luke 12:10: Everyone who speaks a word against the Son of Man will be forgiven, but anyone who blasphemes against the Holy Spirit will not be forgiven.

John 3:5–8: No one can enter the Kingdom of God unless he is born of water and the Spirit. Flesh gives birth to flesh, but the Spirit gives birth to spirit. You should not be surprised at my saying, "You must be born again." The wind blows wherever it pleases. You hear its sound, but you cannot tell where it comes from or where it is going. So it is with everyone born of the Spirit.

John 15:26: When the Counselor comes, whom I will send to you from the Father, the Spirit of truth who goes out from the Father, he will testify about me.

John 16:13–14: When he, the Spirit of truth, comes, he will guide you into all truth. He will not speak on his own; he will speak only what he hears, and he will tell you what is yet to come. He will bring glory to me by taking from what is mine and making it known to you.

## Promises

Matthew 3:11: I baptize you with water for repentance. But after me will come one who is more powerful than I, whose sandals I am not fit to carry. He will baptize you with the Holy Spirit and with fire.

Matthew 10:19–20: When they arrest you, do not worry about what to say or how to say it. At that time you will be given what to say, for it will not be you speaking, but the Spirit of your Father speaking through you.

Luke 11:13: If you then, though you are evil, know how to give good gifts to your children, how much more will your Father in heaven give the Holy Spirit to those who ask him!

Luke 24:49: I am going to send you what my Father has promised; but stay in the city until you have been clothed with power from on high.

John 7:37–39: "If anyone is thirsty, let him come to me and drink. Whoever believes in me, as the Scripture has said, streams of living water will flow from within him." By this [Jesus] meant the Spirit, whom those who believed in him were later to receive. Up to that time the Spirit had not been given, since Jesus had not yet been glorified.

John 14:16–18: I will ask the Father, and he will give you another Counselor to be with you forever—the Spirit of truth. The world cannot accept him, because it neither sees him nor knows him. But you know him, for he lives with you and will be in you. I will not leave you as orphans; I will come to you.

John 14:26: The Counselor, the Holy Spirit, whom the Father will send in my name, will teach you all things and will remind you of everything I have said to you.

John 16:7–11: It is for your good that I am going away. Unless I go away, the Counselor will not come to you; but if I go, I will send him to you. When he comes, he will convict the world of guilt in regard to sin and righteousness and judgment: in regard to sin, because men do not believe in me; in regard to righteousness, because I am going to the Father, where you can see me no longer; and in regard to judgment, because the prince of this world now stands condemned.

## Commands

Matthew 28:19: Go and make disciples of all nations, baptizing them in the name of the Father and of the Son and of the Holy Spirit.

## Reflections

The Holy Spirit is given to us to help us know fully the Lord Jesus Christ. After first giving us life in Christ, the Spirit then guides us into truth. And since Jesus is truth, the Spirit tells us about Jesus. The Spirit tells us, too, of the future, and Jesus is our future. Aiding in discernment, convicting us of sin—so that we can draw nearer to Jesus—informing us of what is right, and telling us how He judges evil, the Holy Spirit identifies us with the Lord Jesus Christ and immerses us in Him. The Spirit lives within us, helping us know what to say and making us fruitful. And the Spirit that does all of this, who will never leave us, is ours for the asking!

# HUMILITY

## Principles

Matthew 11:29: Take my yoke upon you and learn from me, for I am gentle and humble in heart, and you will find rest for your souls.

Matthew 18:4: Whoever humbles himself like this child is the greatest in the kingdom of heaven.

Matthew 21:5: Your king comes to you, gentle and riding on a donkey, on a colt, the foal of a donkey.

Mark 9:35: If anyone wants to be first, he must be the very last, and the servant of all.

Mark 10:31: Many who are first will be last, and the last first.

Mark 10:43–45: Whoever wants to become great among you must be your servant, and whoever wants to be first must be slave of all. For even the Son of Man did not come to be served, but to serve, and to give his life as a ransom for many.

John 6:38: I have come down from heaven not to do my will but to do the will of him who sent me.

## Promises

Matthew 5:3: Blessed are the poor in spirit, for theirs is the kingdom of heaven.

Matthew 5:5: Blessed are the meek, for they will inherit the earth.

Matthew 23:12: Whoever exalts himself will be humbled, and whoever humbles himself will be exalted.

Luke 1:52: He has brought down rulers from their thrones but has lifted up the humble.

## Commands

Matthew 23:8: You are not to be called "Rabbi," for you have only one Master and you are all brothers.

## Reflections

*Humility* is lowliness, that is, freedom from pride. But how do I humble myself? By not considering myself as the master of anyone else. In reality, I am the equal of—no more, no less—every other Christian. I may be more skilled in some area or more mature than other Christians, but that doesn't mean my life has more value.

Humility comes, too, from not attempting to control the life of another person. Rather, humility results in service to others, because it causes one to consider others before oneself.

# HYPOCRISY

## *Principles*

Matthew 6:1: Be careful not to do your "acts of righteousness" before men, to be seen by them. If you do, you will have no reward from your Father in heaven.

Mark 9:49: Everyone will be salted with fire.

Luke 7:35: Wisdom is proved right by all her children.

Luke 8:17: There is nothing hidden that will not be disclosed, and nothing concealed that will not be known or brought out into the open.

Luke 20:46–47: Beware of the teachers of the law. They like to walk around in flowing robes and love to be greeted in the marketplaces and have the most important seats in the synagogues and the places of honor at banquets. They devour widows' houses and for a show make lengthy prayers. Such men will be punished most severely.

John 7:18: He who speaks on his own does so to gain honor for himself, but he who works for the honor of the one who sent him is a man of truth; there is nothing false about him.

John 8:7: If any one of you is without sin, let him be the first to throw a stone at her [the woman caught in adultery].

## Promises

Matthew 23:26: First clean the inside of the cup and dish, and then the outside also will be clean.

## Commands

Matthew 7:5: You hypocrite, first take the plank out of your own eye, and then you will see clearly to remove the speck from your brother's eye.

Matthew 10:26: Do not be afraid of [men]. There is nothing concealed that will not be disclosed, or hidden that will not be made known.

Matthew 23:3: You must obey [the teachers of the law the Pharisees] and do everything they tell you. But do not do what they do, for they do not practice what they preach.

Luke 12:1: Be on your guard against the yeast of the Pharisees, which is hypocrisy.

## Reflections

In the present context, *hypocrisy* means an open display of religion without genuine commitment. The cause of Christ is hurt immeasurably by those who claim to love Christ but who really love only themselves. What they do is for show, because they desire the approval of others.

All acts and motives, however, are known by God, and no act done solely to be seen by people will be rewarded. The approval of people doesn't count. What really counts is God's approval, which comes when the righteous require-ments of the law are fulfilled in us through Christ.

---
I
---

# IDENTIFICATION

## *Principles*

Mark 9:39: No one who does a miracle in my name can in the next moment say anything bad about me, for whoever is not against us is for us.

Luke 9:23: If anyone would come after me, he must deny himself and take up his cross daily and follow me.

## *Promises*

Mark 9:41: Anyone who gives you a cup of water in my name because you belong to Christ will certainly not lose his reward.

Luke 12:8: Whoever acknowledges me before men, the Son of Man will also acknowledge him before the angels of God.

## *Reflections*

When I am rightly identified with Christ, I will do certain things, but I cannot do other things. I cannot, for example, say anything bad about Christ when I have just acted in His name. On the other hand, I do other things naturally. I will happily deny myself, I will happily serve Him, I will happily do for others, I will happily talk about Him.

---
J
---

# JOY

## Principles

John 15:9–11: As the Father has loved me, so have I loved you. Now remain in my love. If you obey my commands, you will remain in my love, just as I have obeyed my Father's commands and remain in his love. I have told you this so that my joy may be in you and that your joy may be complete.

## Promises

Matthew 5:11–12: Blessed are you when people insult you, persecute you and falsely say all kinds of evil against you because of me. Rejoice and be glad, because great is your reward in heaven, for in the same way they persecuted the prophets who were before you.

Luke 6:21: Blessed are you who hunger now, for you will be satisfied. Blessed are you who weep now, for you will laugh.

John 16:24: Until now you have not asked for anything in my name. Ask and you will receive, and your joy will be complete.

John 17:13: I am coming to you [Father] now, but I say these things while I am still in the world, so that they [my disciples] may have the full measure of my joy within them.

## Commands

Luke 10:20: Do not rejoice that the spirits submit to you, but rejoice that your names are written in heaven.

## Reflections

Joy always comes from the Lord. And although the greatest joy comes from knowing that I will spend eternity with Him, I can experience joy in Christ in other ways. I can rejoice in persecution, because I know my reward will come from the Lord. I can be happy because the Lord will satisfy me and produce laughter in me. I can rejoice because the Lord answers my prayers. I can have complete joy in this life because the Lord loves me and has put His life within me. He gives me joy in contemplating the future with Him and in living the present with Him. I can find joy in any circumstance when I use that circumstance to glorify God.

# JUDGING

## Principles

Matthew 7:2: In the same way you judge others, you will be judged, and with the measure you use, it will be measured to you.

Luke 6:42: How can you say to your brother, "Brother, let me take the speck out of your eye," when you yourself fail to see the plank in your own eye? You hypocrite, first take the plank out of your eye, and then you will see clearly to remove the speck from your brother's eye.

John 8:7: If any one of you is without sin, let him be the first to throw a stone at her [the woman caught in adultery].

## Promises

Luke 6:37: Do not judge, and you will not be judged. Do not condemn, and you will not be condemned. Forgive, and you will be forgiven.

## Commands

Matthew 7:1: Do not judge, or you too will be judged.

John 7:24: Stop judging by mere appearances, and make a right judgment.

## Reflections

To understand the true meaning of *judging* in these verses, substitute the phrase *evaluate with a critical spirit*. Whenever I evaluate another with a critical spirit, I, too, will be evaluated in the same way. So I'd better not judge others if I don't want to be judged by them.

The concept is not hard to grasp, but what's difficult is to remove the spirit of criticism that flows so easily from me. To do so requires three things: confessing the sin of judging, asking God to remove the critical spirit from me, and loving the other person. The first two require an act of my will; the third demands what I cannot do (love another person) until I am filled with God's love for me.

## K

# KINGDOM OF GOD

## *Principles*

Matthew 5:20: Unless your righteousness surpasses that of the Pharisees and the teachers of the law, you will certainly not enter the kingdom of heaven.

Matthew 7:21: Not everyone who says to me, "Lord, Lord," will enter the kingdom of heaven, but only he who does the will of my Father who is in heaven.

Matthew 18:3–4: Unless you change and become like little children, you will never enter the kingdom of heaven. Therefore, whoever humbles himself like this child is the greatest in the kingdom of heaven.

Matthew 19:23–24: It is hard for a rich man to enter the kingdom of heaven. Again I tell you, it is easier for a camel to go through the eye of a needle than for a rich man to enter the Kingdom of God.

Luke 8:10: The knowledge of the secrets of the Kingdom of God has been given to you, but to others I speak in parables, so that, "though seeing, they may not see; though hearing, they may not understand."

Luke 17:20–21: The Kingdom of God does not come with your careful observation, nor will people say, "Here it is," or "There it is," because the Kingdom of God is within you.

Luke 18:17: I tell you the truth, anyone who will not receive the Kingdom of God like a little child will never enter it.

John 3:3: No one can see the Kingdom of God unless he is born again.

## Promises

Matthew 6:33: Seek first his kingdom and his righteousness, and all these things [what to eat and drink, what to wear] will be given to you as well.

Matthew 25:34: The King will say to those on his right, "Come, you who are blessed by my Father; take your inheritance, the kingdom prepared for you since the creation of the world."

Luke 6:20: Blessed are you who are poor, for yours is the Kingdom of God.

Luke 22:29: I confer on you a kingdom, just as my Father conferred one on me.

## Commands

Matthew 3:2: Repent, for the kingdom of heaven is near.

Mark 1:15: "The time has come," Jesus said. "The Kingdom of God is near. Repent and believe the good news!"

## Reflections

If a person belongs to the Kingdom of God, it means that God is ruling that person. We do not enter the Kingdom of God by merely saying we are Christians, or by being successful in this life, or by keeping God's law. The way to enter the Kingdom of God is through repentance—turning from doing our own will to doing the Father's will. Along with the act of repentance, we must receive righteousness, which is a gift of God through belief in the atoning work of Christ. In other words, to enter the Kingdom of God, a person must be born again.

# KNOWING GOD

## Principles

Luke 10:22: All things have been committed to me by my Father. No one knows who the Son is except the Father, and no one knows who the Father is except the Son and those to whom the Son chooses to reveal him.

Luke 10:23–24: Blessed are the eyes that see what you see. For I tell you that many prophets and kings wanted to see what you see but did not see it, and to hear what you hear but did not hear it.

John 17:3: This is eternal life: that they may know you, the only true God, and Jesus Christ, whom you have sent.

John 17:17: Sanctify them by the truth; your word is truth.

## Promises

Luke 8:10: The knowledge of the secrets of the Kingdom of God has been given to you, but to others I speak in parables, so that, "though seeing, they may not see; though hearing, they may not understand."

John 17:26: I have made you known to them, and will continue to make you known in order that the love you have for me may be in them and that I myself may be in them.

## Reflections

Eternal life is knowing God. But how do I learn to know Him? Mostly by reading and meditating on His Word. The Word of God not only sanctifies me, it lets me know the character of God. Jesus reveals the character of the Father, and I cannot know the Father except through Jesus. And the only way I learn of Jesus is through the Bible. It makes sense, therefore, to spend much time meditating on the Gospels.

I learn to know God, too, by speaking to Him and watching for the ways He answers.

But the way I know God intimately is by experiencing His love for me, expressed in myriad ways. He tells me the truth. He tells me secrets of what it means to live under His rule. And He gives Jesus to me, to live in me and express His love in the most personal and intimate way.

# L

# LAW

## Principles

Matthew 5:18: Until heaven and earth disappear, not the smallest letter, not the least stroke of a pen, will by any means disappear from the Law until everything is accomplished.

Luke 16:17: It is easier for heaven and earth to disappear than for the least stroke of a pen to drop out of the Law.

John 14:15: If you love me, you will obey what I command.

## Promises

Matthew 5:19: Anyone who breaks one of the least of these commandments and teaches others to do the same will be called least in the kingdom of heaven, but whoever practices and teaches these commands will be called great in the kingdom of heaven.

## Commands

Matthew 22:37–40: "Love the Lord your God with all your heart and with all your soul and with all your mind." This is the first and greatest commandment. And the second is like it: "Love your neighbor as yourself." All the Law and the Prophets hang on these two commandments.

Mark 10:19: You know the commandments: "Do not murder, do not commit adultery, do not steal, do not give false testimony, do not defraud, honor your father and mother."

John 13:34–35: A new command I give you: Love one another. As I have loved you, so you must love one another. By this all men will know that you are my disciples, if you love one another.

## Reflections

One must practice before teaching others. How can I teach something I know nothing about? And how can I become proficient at something until I practice it? How can I teach God's commands before I've practiced them? I will never become great in the kingdom of heaven until I begin to practice God's commandments, because obeying God's commandments is how I show my love for Him. His greatest commandment is that I love Him, and His second greatest commandment is that I love others. My goal, then, should be to practice these two commandments and then teach them to others.

# LEADERSHIP

## Principles

Matthew 10:16–25: I am sending you out like sheep among wolves. Therefore be as shrewd as snakes and as innocent as doves. Be on your guard against men; they will hand you over to the local councils and flog you in their synagogues. On my account you will be brought before governors and kings as witnesses to them and to the Gentiles. But when they arrest you, do not worry about what to say or how to say it. At that time you will be given what to say, for it will not be you speaking, but the Spirit of your Father speaking through you. Brother will betray brother to death, and a father his child; children will rebel against their parents and have them put to death. All men will hate you because of me, but he who stands firm to the end will be saved. When you are persecuted in one place, flee to another. I tell you the truth, you will not finish going through the cities of Israel before the Son of Man comes. A student is not above his teacher, nor a servant above his master. It is enough for the student to be like his teacher, and the servant like his master. If the head of the house has been called Beelzebub, how much more the members of his household!

Matthew 20:26–27: Whoever wants to become great among you must be your servant, and whoever wants to be first must be your slave.

Mark 1:17: Come, follow me, . . . and I will make you fishers of men.

Luke 10:1: After this the Lord appointed seventy-two others and sent them two by two ahead of him to every town and place where he was about to go.

Luke 12:42–44: Who then is the faithful and wise manager, whom the master puts in charge of his servants to give them their food allowance at the proper time? It will be good for that servant whom the master finds doing so when he returns. I tell you the truth, he will put him in charge of all his possessions.

John 13:13–17: You call me "Teacher" and "Lord," and rightly so, for that is what I am. Now that I, your Lord and Teacher, have washed your feet, you also should wash one another's feet. I have set you an example that you should do as I have done for you. I tell you the truth, no servant is greater than his master, nor is a messenger greater than the one who sent him. Now that you know these things, you will be blessed if you do them.

## Promises

Matthew 25:23: Well done, good and faithful servant! You have been faithful with a few things; I will put you in charge of many things. Come and share your master's happiness!

## Commands

There is no command to be a leader!

## Reflections

It's interesting that we are never commanded to be leaders. Many people want to lead, but leadership comes with conditions: one must be willing to be a servant and a slave—not just to God but to other people. Putting all the above verses together—being faithful in serving a few qualifies one to be a servant to many. That's the reward of servanthood, and it is also what constitutes leadership.

But leadership has its risks. You become vulnerable to the evil around you when you step out to lead in the cause of Christ. Many people will hate you and try to destroy your work. So if you identify yourself with Christ and His cause, you will be persecuted as He was.

There is yet another aspect, however, to serving others—doing so actually makes you their leader. You control others, because those whom you serve come under obligation to you unless they are paying you for your services. All giving has some strings attached. Serving others keeps you informed about them, letting you get to know them and become sensitive to their needs. From thus comes the term *servant leader.*

# LIFE

## Principles

Matthew 6:25–34: Therefore I tell you, do not worry about
your life, what you will eat or drink; or about your body,
what you will wear. Is not life more important than food,
and the body more important than clothes? Look at the
birds of the air; they do not sow or reap or store away in
barns, and yet your heavenly Father feeds them. Are you not
much more valuable than they? Who of you by worrying
can add a single hour to his life? And why do you worry
about clothes? See how the lilies of the field grow. They do
not labor or spin. Yet I tell you that not even Solomon in all
his splendor was dressed like one of these. If that is how
God clothes the grass of the field, which is here today and
tomorrow is thrown into the fire, will he not much more
clothe you, O you of little faith? So do not worry, saying,
"What shall we eat?" or "What shall we drink?" or "What
shall we wear?" For the pagans run after all these things, and
your heavenly Father knows that you need them. But seek
first his kingdom and his righteousness, and all these things
will be given to you as well. Therefore do not worry about
tomorrow, for tomorrow will worry about itself. Each day
has enough trouble of its own.

Luke 9:24–25: Whoever wants to save his life will lose it, but
whoever loses his life for me will save it. What good is it for
a man to gain the whole world, and yet lose or forfeit his
very self?

John 6:63: The Spirit gives life; the flesh counts for nothing. The words I have spoken to you are spirit and they are life.

John 12:25: The man who loves his life will lose it, while the man who hates his life in this world will keep it for eternal life.

John 14:6: I am the way and the truth and the life. No one comes to the Father except through me.

## Promises

Luke 20:38: He is not the God of the dead, but of the living, for to him all are alive.

John 6:35: I am the bread of life. He who comes to me will never go hungry, and he who believes in me will never be thirsty.

John 6:57: Just as the living Father sent me and I live because of the Father, so the one who feeds on me will live because of me.

John 10:9–10: I am the gate; whoever enters through me will be saved. He will come in and go out, and find pasture. The thief comes only to steal and kill and destroy; I have come that they may have life, and have it to the full.

## Reflections

The verses here are concerned with life on earth. Eternal life imbues a special quality that begins on earth but is carried on into eternity. The two are closely connected, but not everyone has eternal life. All, however, whether believers or not, have life on earth. Do I want mere existence on earth, or do I want life to the full? The life that is satisfying and content is the life spent with Jesus. The more I am aware of His presence, the fuller my life.

First I am to lose my own life—that is, let go of my own will, my agenda, my rights, and my desires—and surrender them, abandon them, give them over to Jesus. After doing so, I will still think and act, but I won't need to worry about my needs being met. I can spend my time seeking Christ's righteousness and His kingdom on earth, and trust Him to take care of my personal needs.

I am to come to Him, to seek Him, to hunger for Him, and to live each day in faith—that is, believing every word He says to me. Then I will live life to its fullest.

# LIGHT

## Principles

Matthew 5:14–16: You are the light of the world. A city on a hill cannot be hidden. Neither do people light a lamp and put it under a bowl. Instead they put it on its stand, and it gives light to everyone in the house. In the same way, let your light shine before men, that they may see your good deeds and praise your Father in heaven.

Luke 12:2–3: There is nothing concealed that will not be disclosed, or hidden that will not be made known. What you have said in the dark will be heard in the daylight, and what you have whispered in the ear in the inner rooms will be proclaimed from the roofs.

John 3:19–21: This is the verdict: Light has come into the world, but men loved darkness instead of light because their deeds were evil. Everyone who does evil hates the light, and will not come into the light for fear that his deeds will be exposed. But whoever lives by the truth comes into the light, so that it may be seen plainly that what he has done has been done through God.

John 11:9–10: Are there not twelve hours of daylight? A man who walks by day will not stumble, for he sees by this world's light. It is when he walks by night that he stumbles, for he has no light.

## Promises

John 8:12: I am the light of the world. Whoever follows me will never walk in darkness, but will have the light of life.

John 9:5: While I am in the world, I am the light of the world.

John 12:46: I have come into the world as a light, so that no one who believes in me should stay in darkness.

## Commands

Luke 11:35: See to it, then, that the light within you is not darkness.

John 12:35–36: Walk while you have the light, before darkness overtakes you. The man who walks in the dark does not know where he is going. Put your trust in the light while you have it, so that you may become sons of light.

## Reflections

Jesus wants us to have light. And the light He wants us to have is Him. When we become His, He lives within us and makes Himself available to guide our lives. It's exciting to think of having a light within that guides us, and to know that He guides us, too, for the sake of others.

In these verses, Jesus warns us to walk in His light, but we don't always do so. Sooner or later everything we do, say, or think will be exposed to His scrutiny, and we are ashamed. We cannot hide anything from Him. But that's not the end of the story, praise God. If it were, we would constantly live in fear of God's wrath. But Jesus is gracious and He forgives and cleanses. His perfect love casts out our fear.

# LISTENING

## Principles

Matthew 24:35: Heaven and earth will pass away, but my words will never pass away.

Luke 8:18: Consider carefully how you listen. Whoever has will be given more; whoever does not have, even what he thinks he has will be taken from him.

Luke 10:16: He who listens to you listens to me; he who rejects you rejects me; but he who rejects me rejects him who sent me.

Luke 10:42: Only one thing is needed. Mary has chosen what is better, and it will not be taken away from her.

John 8:47: He who belongs to God hears what God says. The reason you do not hear is that you do not belong to God.

## Commands

Mark 4:24: Consider carefully what you hear. . . . With the measure you use, it will be measured to you—and even more.

Mark 9:7: A cloud appeared and enveloped them, and a voice came from the cloud: "This is my Son, whom I love. Listen to him!"

Luke 8:8: He who has ears to hear, let him hear.

Luke 9:35: A voice came from the cloud, saying, "This is my Son, whom I have chosen; listen to him."

## Reflections

Early in the morning, while it's quiet and before I start the day's work, I ask God to speak to me in His Word—and His Word is the one thing that is needed. When He speaks, I must listen, but God says I am also to consider *how* I listen. His specific words through the Scripture will guide my life, and I am to consider them carefully in order to act on them.

# LORD'S SUPPER

## Principles

Luke 22:20: After the supper he took the cup, saying, "This cup is the new covenant in my blood, which is poured out for you."

## Promises

John 6:51: I am the living bread that came down from heaven. If anyone eats of this bread, he will live forever. This bread is my flesh, which I will give for the life of the world.

John 6:53–56: Unless you eat the flesh of the Son of Man and drink his blood, you have no life in you. Whoever eats my flesh and drinks my blood has eternal life, and I will raise him up at the last day. For my flesh is real food and my blood is real drink. Whoever eats my flesh and drinks my blood remains in me, and I in him.

## Commands

Matthew 26:26–29: While they were eating, Jesus took bread, gave thanks and broke it, and gave it to his disciples, saying, "Take and eat; this is my body." Then he took the cup, gave thanks and offered it to them, saying, "Drink from it, all of you. This is my blood of the covenant, which is poured out for many for the forgiveness of sins. I tell you, I will not drink of this fruit of the vine from now on until that day when I drink it anew with you in my Father's kingdom."

Luke 22:17: After taking the cup, he gave thanks and said, "Take this and divide it among you."

Luke 22:19: He took bread, gave thanks and broke it, and gave it to them, saying, "This is my body given for you; do this in remembrance of me."

## Reflections

The Lord's Supper is the sacramental meal of God's people. The Lord Jesus provided it for us as an illustration of how He becomes a part of us. The sacrament reminds us that it's not enough just to believe certain facts about Jesus. We must believe Him and receive His person into our bodies. The apostle John is clear about the necessity of receiving Christ: "Unless you eat the flesh of the Son of Man and drink his blood, you have no life in you." The Lord's Supper reminds us that we have done so, and that now, having the Lord Himself one with us, we live out His life.

The promise is plain and wonderful—"Whoever eats my flesh and drinks my blood remains in me, and I in him"!

# LOVE

## *Principles*

Matthew 10:37: Anyone who loves his father or mother more than me is not worthy of me; anyone who loves his son or daughter more than me is not worthy of me.

Luke 7:47: Her [the woman who lived a sinful life] many sins have been forgiven—for she loved much. But he who has been forgiven little loves little.

John 8:42: If God were your Father, you would love me, for I came from God and now am here. I have not come on my own; but he sent me.

John 14:15: If you love me, you will obey what I command.

John 15:13: Greater love has no one than this, that he lay down his life for his friends.

John 16:27: The Father himself loves you because you have loved me and have believed that I came from God.

John 21:15–17: When they had finished eating, Jesus said to Simon Peter, "Simon son of John, do you truly love me more than these?" "Yes, Lord," he said, "you know that I love you." Jesus said, "Feed my lambs." Again Jesus said, "Simon son of John, do you truly love me?" He answered, "Yes, Lord, you know that I love you." Jesus said, "Take care of my sheep." The third time he said to him, "Simon son of

John, do you love me?" Peter was hurt because Jesus asked him the third time, "Do you love me?" He said, "Lord, you know all things; you know that I love you." Jesus said, "Feed my sheep."

## Promises

John 13:34–35: A new command I give you: Love one another. As I have loved you, so you must love one another. By this all men will know that you are my disciples, if you love one another.

John 14:21: Whoever has my commands and obeys them, he is the one who loves me. He who loves me will be loved by my Father, and I too will love him and show myself to him.

John 14:23: If anyone loves me, he will obey my teaching. My Father will love him, and we will come to him and make our home with him.

## Commands

Matthew 5:43–45: You have heard that it was said, "Love your neighbor and hate your enemy." But I tell you: Love your enemies and pray for those who persecute you, that you may be sons of your Father in heaven. He causes his sun to rise on the evil and the good, and sends rain on the righteous and the unrighteous.

Matthew 22:37–40: "Love the Lord your God with all your heart and with all your soul and with all your mind." This is the first and greatest commandment. And the second is like it: "Love your neighbor as yourself." All the Law and the Prophets hang on these two commandments.

John 13:34: A new command I give you: Love one another. As I have loved you, so you must love one another.

John 15:9–10: As the Father has loved me, so have I loved you. Now remain in my love. If you obey my commands, you will remain in my love, just as I have obeyed my Father's commands and remain in his love.

John 15:12: My command is this: Love each other as I have loved you.

## Reflections

Loving God and loving others go hand in hand. Jesus commanded both. But the sequence is this: God loves me—I love Him—then I love others—and I can, even if they don't love me.

# LOVING GOD

## Principles

Matthew 25:40: Whatever you did for one of the least of these brothers of mine, you did for me.

John 8:42: If God were your Father, you would love me, for I came from God and now am here. I have not come on my own; but he sent me.

John 12:8: You will always have the poor among you, but you will not always have me.

John 16:27: The Father himself loves you because you have loved me and have believed that I came from God.

John 21:15–17: When they had finished eating, Jesus said to Simon Peter, "Simon son of John, do you truly love me more than these?" "Yes, Lord," he said, "you know that I love you." Jesus said, "Feed my lambs." Again Jesus said, "Simon son of John, do you truly love me?" He answered, "Yes, Lord, you know that I love you." Jesus said, "Take care of my sheep." The third time he said to him, "Simon son of John, do you love me?" Peter was hurt because Jesus asked him the third time, "Do you love me?" He said, "Lord, you know all things; you know that I love you." Jesus said, "Feed my sheep.

## Promises

John 14:21: Whoever has my commands and obeys them, he is the one who loves me. He who loves me will be loved by my Father, and I too will love him and show myself to him.

John 14:23: If anyone loves me, he will obey my teaching. My Father will love him, and we will come to him and make our home with him.

## Commands

Matthew 10:37: Anyone who loves his father or mother more than me is not worthy of me; anyone who loves his son or daughter more than me is not worthy of me.

Mark 12:30: Love the Lord your God with all your heart and with all your soul and with all your mind and with all your strength.

John 14:15: If you love me, you will obey what I command.

John 14:21: Whoever has my commands and obeys them, he is the one who loves me. He who loves me will be loved by my Father, and I too will love him and show myself to him.

John 14:23–24: If anyone loves me, he will obey my teaching. My Father will love him, and we will come to him and make our home with him. He who does not love me will not obey my teaching. These words you hear are not my own; they belong to the Father who sent me.

John 15:9–11: As the Father has loved me, so have I loved you. Now remain in my love. If you obey my commands, you will remain in my love, just as I have obeyed my Father's commands and remain in his love. I have told you this so that my joy may be in you and that your joy may be complete.

## Reflections

I am to love God with all my heart. The state of the heart, however, is related to the will; I must *will* to love God. I'm motivated to love Him, because He first loved me. When I set my will to love Him back, then my soul (emotions), mind, and strength (body) follow. But I must first make the choice to love Him, then comes the outworking. If I start with the outworking, I become legalistic and discouraged. Free outworking, then, begins with my asking God to reveal His love in such a way that I will to love Him in return.

Jesus provides the revelation of God's love. Jesus tells me that He loves me as the Father has loved Him. How does the Father love Jesus? By providing for Him, guiding His life, giving Him the ultimate in purpose and usefulness, and by maintaining a personal relationship of love that brings security, joy, and satisfaction. This is the way that Jesus loves me. It is up to me to respond to His love, and I respond by obeying His commands.

# M

# MARRIAGE

## *Principles*

Matthew 19:5: For this reason a man will leave his father and mother and be united to his wife, and the two will become one flesh.

Matthew 19:9: Anyone who divorces his wife, except for marital unfaithfulness, and marries another woman commits adultery.

Mark 12:25: When the dead rise, they will neither marry nor be given in marriage; they will be like the angels in heaven.

Luke 20:34–35: The people of this age marry and are given in marriage. But those who are considered worthy of taking part in that age and in the resurrection from the dead will neither marry nor be given in marriage

## *Commands*

Matthew 19:6: So [husband and wife] are no longer two, but one. Therefore what God has joined together, let man not separate.

## Reflections

The choice to marry is the choice to no longer remain a private individual. That's why marriage is for this life only and not for heaven. In heaven we'll be joined only with Christ, and our focus will be on Him alone. God has made provision for this life, however, and humans are never to violate God's provision of one man for one woman.

# MERCY

## *Principles*

Matthew 18:23–35: The kingdom of heaven is like a king who wanted to settle accounts with his servants. As he began the settlement, a man who owed him ten thousand talents was brought to him. Since he was not able to pay, the master ordered that he and his wife and his children and all that he had be sold to repay the debt. The servant fell on his knees before him. "Be patient with me," he begged, "and I will pay back everything." The servant's master took pity on him, canceled the debt and let him go. But when that servant went out, he found one of his fellow servants who owed him a hundred denarii. He grabbed him and began to choke him. "Pay back what you owe me!" he demanded. His fellow servant fell to his knees and begged him, "Be patient with me, and I will pay you back." But he refused. Instead, he went off and had the man thrown into prison until he could pay the debt. When the other servants saw what had happened, they were greatly distressed and went and told their master everything that had happened. Then the master called the servant in. "You wicked servant," he said, "I canceled all that debt of yours because you begged me to. Shouldn't you have had mercy on your fellow servant just as I had on you?" In anger his master turned him over to the jailers to be tortured, until he should pay back all he owed. This is how my heavenly Father will treat each of you unless you forgive your brother from your heart.

## Promises

Matthew 5:7: Blessed are the merciful, for they will be shown mercy.

Matthew 12:20: A bruised reed he will not break, and a smoldering wick he will not snuff out, till he leads justice to victory.

## Commands

Matthew 9:13: Go and learn what this means: "I desire mercy, not sacrifice." For I have not come to call the righteous, but sinners.

Luke 6:36: Be merciful, just as your Father is merciful.

Luke 10:30–37: "A man was going down from Jerusalem to Jericho, when he fell into the hands of robbers. They stripped him of his clothes, beat him and went away, leaving him half dead. A priest happened to be going down the same road, and when he saw the man, he passed by on the other side. So too, a Levite, when he came to the place and saw him, passed by on the other side. But a Samaritan, as he traveled, came where the man was; and when he saw him, he took pity on him. He went to him and bandaged his wounds, pouring on oil and wine. Then he put the man on his own donkey, took him to an inn and took care of him. The next day he took out two silver coins and gave them to the innkeeper. 'Look after him,' he said, 'and when I return, I will reimburse you for any extra expense you may have.' Which of these three do you think was a neighbor to the man who fell into the hands of robbers?" The expert in the law replied, "The one who had mercy on him." Jesus told him, "Go and do likewise."

## Reflections

*Mercy* is undeserved kindness and compassion.

God is merciful. He is not mean and callous—He finds no delight in allowing a person to be brought to his or her knees just to show His righteousness. He calls to Him those who have sinned, those who hurt desperately, those who are troubled. That's what God's mercy means. I, too, am to show mercy by looking at those around me. Which ones need me and want my help? It is those I am to tenderly lift up in a way that will strengthen them.

But the greatest way I can show mercy is by forgiving. Those who have wronged me need forgiveness, and I will be tortured in my self-made prison until I demonstrate mercy to them. God has shown mercy on me and forgiven me for far greater sins than those committed against me.

# MIND

## Principles

Matthew 12:34: You brood of vipers, how can you who are evil say anything good? For out of the overflow of the heart the mouth speaks.

Matthew 16:23: Jesus turned and said to Peter, "Get behind me, Satan! You are a stumbling block to me; you do not have in mind the things of God, but the things of men."

Mark 7:21: For from within, out of men's hearts, come evil thoughts, sexual immorality, theft, murder, adultery.

Luke 1:51: He has performed mighty deeds with his arm; he has scattered those who are proud in their inmost thoughts.

Luke 24:38: Why are you troubled, and why do doubts rise in your minds?

## Promises

Luke 24:45: Then he opened their minds so they could understand the Scriptures.

## Commands

Matthew 22:37: Love the Lord your God with all your heart and with all your soul and with all your mind.

## Reflections

We use our minds to think through the issues of life and to come to conclusions. The mind controls us because it determines our will—as we think, so we act. It makes sense, then, to control carefully what goes into the mind and what we allow to stay there. Satan does his greatest damage through the control of the mind, and he practices deception by placing his lies in minds that are open to him.

# MISSION

## Principles

Matthew 9:37: The harvest is plentiful but the workers are few.

Matthew 10:8: Freely you have received, freely give.

Matthew 10:14: If anyone will not welcome you or listen to your words, shake the dust off your feet when you leave that home or town.

Matthew 21:43: The Kingdom of God will be taken away from you and given to a people who will produce its fruit.

John 4:36–37: Even now the reaper draws his wages, even now he harvests the crop for eternal life, so that the sower and the reaper may be glad together. Thus the saying "One sows and another reaps" is true.

John 17:18: As you sent me into the world, I have sent them into the world.

## Promises

Matthew 4:19: Come, follow me, . . . and I will make you fishers of men.

Matthew 28:18–20: All authority in heaven and on earth has been given to me. Therefore go and make disciples of all nations, baptizing them in the name of the Father and of the Son and of the Holy Spirit, and teaching them to obey everything I have commanded you. And surely I am with you always, to the very end of the age.

Luke 5:10: Don't be afraid; from now on you will catch men.

John 4:38: I sent you to reap what you have not worked for. Others have done the hard work, and you have reaped the benefits of their labor.

## Commands

Matthew 4:19: Come, follow me, . . . and I will make you fishers of men.

Matthew 10:27: What I tell you in the dark, speak in the daylight; what is whispered in your ear, proclaim from the roofs.

Matthew 28:19–20: Go and make disciples of all nations, baptizing them in the name of the Father and of the Son and of the Holy Spirit, and teaching them to obey everything I have commanded you.

Mark 16:15: Go into all the world and preach the good news to all creation.

Luke 9:60: Let the dead bury their own dead, but you go and proclaim the Kingdom of God.

Luke 10:2: The harvest is plentiful, but the workers are few. Ask the Lord of the harvest, therefore, to send out workers into his harvest field.

Luke 10:3: Go! I am sending you out like lambs among wolves.

Luke 14:23: Go out to the roads and country lanes and make them come in, so that my house will be full.

John 4:35: Do you not say, "Four months more and then the harvest"? I tell you, open your eyes and look at the fields! They are ripe for harvest.

John 20:21: Peace be with you! As the Father has sent me, I am sending you.

## Reflections

The command is to follow Jesus. The promise is that when I do, I will bring people to Christ. To follow Christ means to live as He did—a life of solitude, simplicity, service, and communion with His Father. The results of living that kind of life are up to Christ. He will see that I attract others to Him, and it will be as easy as living and breathing.

# O

# OBEDIENCE

## *Principles*

Matthew 7:21: Not everyone who says to me, "Lord, Lord," will enter the kingdom of heaven, but only he who does the will of my Father who is in heaven.

Luke 11:28: Blessed rather are those who hear the word of God and obey it.

John 14:15: If you love me, you will obey what I command.

John 14:21: Whoever has my commands and obeys them, he is the one who loves me. He who loves me will be loved by my Father, and I too will love him and show myself to him.

John 14:23–24: If anyone loves me, he will obey my teaching. My Father will love him, and we will come to him and make our home with him. He who does not love me will not obey my teaching. These words you hear are not my own; they belong to the Father who sent me.

## *Promises*

Matthew 12:50: Whoever does the will of my Father in heaven is my brother and sister and mother.

John 8:51: I tell you the truth, if anyone keeps my word, he will never see death.

## Commands

John 5:14: You are well again. Stop sinning or something worse may happen to you.

## Reflections

True obedience issues from a heart of love, because love wants to do the will of its object. Because Jesus did the will of His Father out of love for Him, then I am kin to Jesus when I, too, choose to do the will of our Father. But obedience is more than just *wanting* to do the will of God; obedience is the practice of doing God's will.

Jesus learned obedience and so, too, must I. I do so by choosing a starting point, and disciplining myself to certain actions that conform to the will of God for me. Spontaneous obedience comes from practice. The more I practice obeying God the more I will obey Him spontaneously. Obedience, then, is related to application (see "Application" in this volume).

# OPPOSITION

## Principles

Matthew 5:43–45: You have heard that it was said, "Love your neighbor and hate your enemy." But I tell you: Love your enemies and pray for those who persecute you, that you may be sons of your Father in heaven. He causes his sun to rise on the evil and the good, and sends rain on the righteous and the unrighteous.

Matthew 10:34–36: Do not suppose that I have come to bring peace to the earth. I did not come to bring peace, but a sword. For I have come to turn "a man against his father, a daughter against her mother, a daughter-in-law against her mother-in-law—a man's enemies will be the members of his own household."

Luke 20:43: I [will] make your enemies a footstool for your feet.

## Promises

Matthew 10:22: All men will hate you because of me, but he who stands firm to the end will be saved.

Luke 6:35: Love your enemies, do good to them, and lend to them without expecting to get anything back. Then your reward will be great, and you will be sons of the Most High, because he is kind to the ungrateful and wicked.

## Commands

Luke 6:27: Love your enemies, do good to those who hate you.

## Reflections

As Christians, we must expect opposition. But opposition is not simply the inevitable result of being a Christian; Jesus actually initiates it in our lives. Why would He do that? Consider that it's only through conflict that we grow, that God can be glorified most when we deal with conflict in His power, that conflicts in relationships force us to do the only thing important in life—to love. Jesus loved us while we were His enemies, and we are to love our enemies—do good to those who persecute us, forgive those who abuse us. If spiritual growth, glorifying God, and learning to love are valid reasons for opposition, then we should thank Him for the conflict we experience and trust God to use it for our benefit and for His glory.

---
P
---

# PARENTS

## *Principles*

Matthew 10:37: Anyone who loves his father or mother more than me is not worthy of me.

Luke 14:26: If anyone comes to me and does not hate his father and mother, his wife and children, his brothers and sisters—yes, even his own life—he cannot be my disciple.

## *Commands*

Matthew 8:22: Follow me, and let the dead bury their own dead.

Matthew 15:4: For God said, "Honor your father and mother" and "Anyone who curses his father or mother must be put to death."

Mark 10:19: You know the commandments: "Do not murder, do not commit adultery, do not steal, do not give false testimony, do not defraud, honor your father and mother."

## *Reflections*

Honoring parents (or anyone) never means putting them before obedience to God. But putting God first doesn't mean that I should not honor my parents. Honoring God

and honoring others is never "either/or;" it's always "both."
A way that I show honor to God, in fact, is by honoring
others more than myself.

# PEACE

## Principles

Matthew 10:34: Do not suppose that I have come to bring peace to the earth. I did not come to bring peace, but a sword.

John 16:33: I have told you these things, so that in me you may have peace. In this world you will have trouble. But take heart! I have overcome the world.

## Promises

Matthew 5:9: Blessed are the peacemakers, for they will be called sons of God.

Luke 24:36: While they were still talking about this, Jesus himself stood among them and said to them, "Peace be with you."

John 20:19: On the evening of that first day of the week, when the disciples were together, with the doors locked for fear of the Jews, Jesus came and stood among them and said, "Peace be with you!"

## Commands

John 14:27: Peace I leave with you; my peace I give you. I do not give to you as the world gives. Do not let your hearts be troubled and do not be afraid.

## Reflections

Peace is not simply absence of conflict; peace is resolution with God, which leads to wholeness and well-being in all areas of life. Jesus says His children can have peace even in the midst of trouble. But such is not the case for unbelievers. For them, there is no peace but a sword. The beginning point of peace comes from understanding, so where there is confusion, there can be no peace. But when we listen to the Word of God, the Holy Spirit will give understanding.

# PERSECUTION

## *Principles*

Matthew 12:30: He who is not with me is against me, and he who does not gather with me scatters.

Matthew 24:9: You will be handed over to be persecuted and put to death, and you will be hated by all nations because of me.

Mark 6:4: Only in his hometown, among his relatives and in his own house is a prophet without honor.

Mark 6:11: If any place will not welcome you or listen to you, shake the dust off your feet when you leave, as a testimony against them.

Luke 10:16: He who listens to you listens to me; he who rejects you rejects me; but he who rejects me rejects him who sent me.

Luke 16:31: If they do not listen to Moses and the Prophets, they will not be convinced even if someone rises from the dead.

John 15:18–21: If the world hates you, keep in mind that it hated me first. If you belonged to the world, it would love you as its own. As it is, you do not belong to the world, but I have chosen you out of the world. That is why the world hates you. Remember the words I spoke to you: "No servant is greater than his master." If they persecuted me, they will persecute you also. If they obeyed my teaching, they will obey yours also. They will treat you this way because of my name, for they do not know the One who sent me.

John 16:1–4: All this I have told you so that you will not go astray. They will put you out of the synagogue; in fact, a time is coming when anyone who kills you will think he is offering a service to God. They will do such things because they have not known the Father or me. I have told you this, so that when the time comes you will remember that I warned you. I did not tell you this at first because I was with you.

## Promises

Matthew 5:10–12: Blessed are those who are persecuted because of righteousness, for theirs is the kingdom of heaven. Blessed are you when people insult you, persecute you and falsely say all kinds of evil against you because of me. Rejoice and be glad, because great is your reward in heaven, for in the same way they persecuted the prophets who were before you.

Mark 13:13: All men will hate you because of me, but he who stands firm to the end will be saved.

## Commands

Matthew 5:44: Love your enemies and pray for those who persecute you.

Matthew 10:23: When you are persecuted in one place, flee to another.

Luke 23:34: Jesus said, "Father, forgive them, for they do not know what they are doing." And they divided up his clothes by casting lots.

## Reflections

In the present context, *persecution* is oppression because of one's faith. Jesus had much to say about persecution, because it was a reality in His own life and would, therefore, be a reality in the lives of His followers. Persecution will come even from the places where it should not—namely, our own homes and families—causing more pain than any other source of persecution. Jesus says, however, that persecution should give me joy because it identifies me with Him, and I will thus receive a reward in heaven. Although I do not pray for persecution, I will rejoice when it comes.

But I'm to do more than rejoice over persecution. I am to love those who persecute me, praying that they will repent, wanting them to be reconciled to God for their sakes and for His.

# PERSEVERANCE

## Principles

John 10:27–29: My sheep listen to my voice; I know them, and they follow me. I give them eternal life, and they shall never perish; no one can snatch them out of my hand. My Father, who has given them to me, is greater than all; no one can snatch them out of my Father's hand.

## Promises

Matthew 24:12–13: Because of the increase of wickedness, the love of most will grow cold, but he who stands firm to the end will be saved.

John 6:37: All that the Father gives me will come to me, and whoever comes to me I will never drive away.

## Reflections

*Perseverance* means to remain firm in our faith. But we do so only because the Lord has promised that He will never reject His own, nor will He allow anyone to take them out of His hand. It's comforting to know that our perseverance doesn't depend upon us; it depends upon the keeping power of the Holy Spirit, who lives within us. Our love may wax and wane, but we are able to stand firm because we are the Lord's sheep, given to Jesus by His Father and kept by the Holy Spirit.

# PRAYER

## Principles

Mark 1:35: Very early in the morning, while it was still dark, Jesus got up, left the house and went off to a solitary place, where he prayed.

Mark 9:29: This kind can come out only by prayer.

Luke 18:7: Will not God bring about justice for his chosen ones, who cry out to him day and night? Will he keep putting them off?

John 9:31: We know that God does not listen to sinners. He listens to the godly man who does his will.

## Promises

Matthew 6:6: When you pray, go into your room, close the door and pray to your Father, who is unseen. Then your Father, who sees what is done in secret, will reward you.

Matthew 7:7–8: Ask and it will be given to you; seek and you will find; knock and the door will be opened to you. For everyone who asks receives; he who seeks finds; and to him who knocks, the door will be opened.

Matthew 7:11: If you, then, though you are evil, know how to give good gifts to your children, how much more will your Father in heaven give good gifts to those who ask him!

Matthew 18:19–20: If two of you on earth agree about anything you ask for, it will be done for you by my Father in heaven. For where two or three come together in my name, there am I with them.

Mark 11:23–25: If anyone says to this mountain, "Go, throw yourself into the sea," and does not doubt in his heart but believes that what he says will happen, it will be done for him. Therefore I tell you, whatever you ask for in prayer, believe that you have received it, and it will be yours. And when you stand praying, if you hold anything against anyone, forgive him, so that your Father in heaven may forgive you your sins.

John 14:13–14: I will do whatever you ask in my name, so that the Son may bring glory to the Father. You may ask me for anything in my name, and I will do it.

John 15:7: If you remain in me and my words remain in you, ask whatever you wish, and it will be given you.

John 15:16: You did not choose me, but I chose you and appointed you to go and bear fruit—fruit that will last. Then the Father will give you whatever you ask in my name.

John 16:23–24: In that day you will no longer ask me anything. I tell you the truth, my Father will give you whatever you ask in my name. Until now you have not asked for anything in my name. Ask and you will receive, and your joy will be complete.

## Commands

Matthew 9:38: Ask the Lord of the harvest, therefore, to send out workers into his harvest field.

Matthew 26:41: Watch and pray so that you will not fall into temptation. The spirit is willing, but the body is weak.

## Reflections

*Prayer* is communication with God. And because it is a privilege and not a requirement, Jesus doesn't give many commands in regard to prayer. He does, however, give a lot of promises. Note, too, that nowhere is an unbeliever admonished to pray. Prayer is reserved for believers, for God's children who will receive good gifts from Him when they ask. God, however, does not always immediately answer His children's prayers. Sometimes He waits in order to increase our faith. Sometimes He waits in order to make us persevere. And sometimes He waits in order to make our attitudes what they should be. It seems that most often, however, He waits until the request is entirely in line with His will.

# PRIORITIES

## Principles

Matthew 6:21: Where your treasure is, there your heart will be also.

Matthew 10:37: Anyone who loves his father or mother more than me is not worthy of me; anyone who loves his son or daughter more than me is not worthy of me.

Matthew 22:37–40: "Love the Lord your God with all your heart and with all your soul and with all your mind." This is the first and greatest commandment. And the second is like it: "Love your neighbor as yourself." All the Law and the Prophets hang on these two commandments.

Mark 14:7: The poor you will always have with you, and you can help them any time you want. But you will not always have me.

Luke 9:24–25: Whoever wants to save his life will lose it, but whoever loses his life for me will save it. What good is it for a man to gain the whole world, and yet lose or forfeit his very self?

## Promises

Matthew 6:33: Seek first his kingdom and his righteousness, and all these things will be given to you as well.

## Commands

Matthew 4:10: Worship the Lord your God, and serve him only.

Matthew 8:22: Follow me, and let the dead bury their own dead.

Matthew 22:21: Give to Caesar what is Caesar's, and to God what is God's.

Matthew 23:8–10: You are not to be called "Rabbi," for you have only one Master and you are all brothers. And do not call anyone on earth "father," for you have one Father, and he is in heaven. Nor are you to be called "teacher," for you have one Teacher, the Christ.

Mark 12:30–31: "Love the Lord your God with all your heart and with all your soul and with all your mind and with all your strength." . . . "Love your neighbor as yourself." There is no commandment greater than these.

Luke 9:60: Let the dead bury their own dead, but you go and proclaim the Kingdom of God.

Luke 12:31: Seek his kingdom, and these things will be given to you as well.

## Reflections

God has made His priorities clear. Nothing is to come before Him—no cause, no people, not even family. I am to worship God, serve Him only, follow Him, give to Him what belongs to Him—namely myself. God's priorities include calling no one *Father*—meaning the One who provides and protects. Nor should I allow anyone to look to me instead of to God as their master or teacher.

Further, I am to seek Christ's kingdom above any other kingdom, and I am to proclaim that kingdom to others.

I am first, then, to love God with all that is in me, and I am also to love other people. If I follow these priorities, I will have a life totally wrapped up in the Lord. Other worthwhile causes will deserve my support, but they will not consume my interest.

---
R
---

# READINESS

## Principles

Matthew 24:44: You also must be ready, because the Son of Man will come at an hour when you do not expect him.

Luke 12:37–38: It will be good for those servants whose master finds them watching when he comes. I tell you the truth, he will dress himself to serve, will have them recline at the table and will come and wait on them. It will be good for those servants whose master finds them ready, even if he comes in the second or third watch of the night.

## Promises

Luke 12:42–43: Who then is the faithful and wise manager, whom the master puts in charge of his servants to give them their food allowance at the proper time? It will be good for that servant whom the master finds doing so when he returns.

## Commands

Matthew 24:42: Keep watch, because you do not know on what day your Lord will come.

Matthew 25:13: Keep watch, because you do not know the day or the hour.

Matthew 26:41: Watch and pray so that you will not fall into temptation. The spirit is willing, but the body is weak.

Luke 12:35–36: Be dressed ready for service and keep your lamps burning, like men waiting for their master to return from a wedding banquet, so that when he comes and knocks they can immediately open the door for him.

Luke 12:39–40: If the owner of the house had known at what hour the thief was coming, he would not have let his house be broken into. You also must be ready, because the Son of Man will come at an hour when you do not expect him.

John 12:36: Put your trust in the light while you have it, so that you may become sons of light.

## Reflections

I must be ready when my Lord comes back for me. And no matter how old I am, that doesn't give me much time. I become ready not so much by being prepared as by keeping watch for Him—watching not only for His return but watching for Him in everything. If I keep watching, then on the day He actually appears, He will be familiar to me, and He will be the fulfillment of my expectations.

# RECONCILIATION

## Principles

Matthew 5:23–24: If you are offering your gift at the altar and there remember that your brother has something against you, leave your gift there in front of the altar. First go and be reconciled to your brother; then come and offer your gift.

Matthew 18:15–17: If your brother sins against you, go and show him his fault, just between the two of you. If he listens to you, you have won your brother over. But if he will not listen, take one or two others along, so that "every matter may be established by the testimony of two or three witnesses." If he refuses to listen to them, tell it to the church; and if he refuses to listen even to the church, treat him as you would a pagan or a tax collector.

## Promises

John 17:11: I will remain in the world no longer, but [these whom you gave me] are still in the world, and I am coming to you. Holy Father, protect them by the power of your name—the name you gave me—so that they may be one as we are one.

John 17:22–23: I have given them the glory that you gave me, that they may be one as we are one: I in them and you in me. May they be brought to complete unity to let the world know that you sent me and have loved them even as you have loved me.

## Commands

Matthew 5:25: Settle matters quickly with your adversary who is taking you to court. Do it while you are still with him on the way, or he may hand you over to the judge, and the judge may hand you over to the officer, and you may be thrown into prison.

Luke 12:58: As you are going with your adversary to the magistrate, try hard to be reconciled to him on the way, or he may drag you off to the judge, and the judge turn you over to the officer, and the officer throw you into prison.

## Reflections

Reconciliation is always my responsibility. Whether another person offends me or whether I offend another person, I am still responsible to initiate the reconciliation. And I am to do it quickly. The Lord wants me to live in complete unity with my brothers and sisters so that the world will know that Jesus came to love and unify Christians.

# RELATIONS WITH OTHERS

## Principles

Matthew 10:40: He who receives you receives me, and he who receives me receives the one who sent me.

Matthew 13:57: Only in his hometown and in his own house is a prophet without honor.

Matthew 18:15–17: If your brother sins against you, go and show him his fault, just between the two of you. If he listens to you, you have won your brother over. But if he will not listen, take one or two others along, so that "every matter may be established by the testimony of two or three witnesses." If he refuses to listen to them, tell it to the church; and if he refuses to listen even to the church, treat him as you would a pagan or a tax collector.

Luke 6:26: Woe to you when all men speak well of you, for that is how their fathers treated the false prophets.

Luke 6:31: Do to others as you would have them do to you.

## Promises

Luke 6:35: Love your enemies, do good to them, and lend to them without expecting to get anything back. Then your reward will be great, and you will be sons of the Most High, because he is kind to the ungrateful and wicked.

Luke 6:37: Do not judge, and you will not be judged. Do not condemn, and you will not be condemned. Forgive, and you will be forgiven.

Luke 6:38: Give, and it will be given to you. A good measure, pressed down, shaken together and running over, will be poured into your lap. For with the measure you use, it will be measured to you.

## Commands

Matthew 5:41: If someone forces you to go one mile, go with him two miles.

Matthew 5:42: Give to the one who asks you, and do not turn away from the one who wants to borrow from you.

Matthew 22:39: Love your neighbor as yourself.

Mark 9:50: Salt is good, but if it loses its saltiness, how can you make it salty again? Have salt in yourselves, and be at peace with each other.

Luke 6:29–30: If someone strikes you on one cheek, turn to him the other also. If someone takes your cloak, do not stop him from taking your tunic. Give to everyone who asks you, and if anyone takes what belongs to you, do not demand it back.

Luke 6:36: Be merciful, just as your Father is merciful.

## Reflections

The one great principle of getting along with others is "Do to others as you would have them do to you." Jesus made wonderful promises, however, for those who would do *better* to others than they would do to you. Loving enemies rather than merely tolerating them, doing good to them rather than ignoring them, giving to them rather than demanding payment from them, giving without expecting any thanks, and forgiving them (when they have repented of offenses against you) will bring the great reward of being like God.

# RELATIONSHIP WITH GOD

## *Principles*

Matthew 18:3: Unless you change and become like little children, you will never enter the kingdom of heaven.

Mark 9:39–40: No one who does a miracle in my name can in the next moment say anything bad about me, for whoever is not against us is for us.

John 5:22–23: The Father judges no one, but has entrusted all judgment to the Son, that all may honor the Son just as they honor the Father. He who does not honor the Son does not honor the Father, who sent him.

John 6:53: Unless you eat the flesh of the Son of Man and drink his blood, you have no life in you.

John 6:65: This is why I told you that no one can come to me unless the Father has enabled him.

John 8:47: He who belongs to God hears what God says. The reason you do not hear is that you do not belong to God.

John 13:8: Unless I wash you, you have no part with me.

John 14:6–7: I am the way and the truth and the life. No one comes to the Father except through me. If you really knew me, you would know my Father as well. From now on, you do know him and have seen him.

John 16:27: The Father himself loves you because you have loved me and have believed that I came from God.

# Promises

Matthew 10:40: He who receives you receives me, and he who receives me receives the one who sent me.

Mark 3:35: Whoever does God's will is my brother and sister and mother.

Luke 9:48: Whoever welcomes this little child in my name welcomes me; and whoever welcomes me welcomes the one who sent me. For he who is least among you all—he is the greatest.

John 5:24: Whoever hears my word and believes him who sent me has eternal life and will not be condemned; he has crossed over from death to life.

John 6:56: Whoever eats my flesh and drinks my blood remains in me, and I in him.

John 12:32: But I, when I am lifted up from the earth, will draw all men to myself.

John 14:9: Anyone who has seen me has seen the Father.

John 14:23: If anyone loves me, he will obey my teaching. My Father will love him, and we will come to him and make our home with him.

John 15:14–15: You are my friends if you do what I command. I no longer call you servants, because a servant does not know his master's business. Instead, I have called you friends, for everything that I learned from my Father I have made known to you.

John 17:25–26: Father, . . . I have made you known to [those you have given me], and will continue to make you known in order that the love you have for me may be in them and that I myself may be in them.

## Commands

Matthew 5:48: Be perfect, therefore, as your heavenly Father is perfect.

Matthew 7:13: Enter through the narrow gate. For wide is the gate and broad is the road that leads to destruction, and many enter through it.

Matthew 10:28: Do not be afraid of those who kill the body but cannot kill the soul. Rather, be afraid of the One who can destroy both soul and body in hell.

## Reflections

My relationship with God begins with Him—He chooses me. But only through Jesus can I have a relationship with God, so He gives me faith to believe in Jesus, thereby making me His child. When Jesus enters my being, God the Father and God the Holy Spirit enter as well. Therefore, I would be wise to develop my relationship with Jesus, because to know Jesus is to know God.

I learn to know Him through reading the Scriptures (especially the Gospels) and by prayer, and I honor Him by partaking of His flesh and of His blood. I honor Him, too, by listening to what He says, believing it as truth, obeying Him, and loving Him with all my heart.

Although my relationship begins with God, it is not dependent upon doing God's will. The result of a relationship with God, however, will be the desire to do God's will (read John 3).

# REPENTANCE

## Principles

Matthew 3:8: Produce fruit in keeping with repentance.

Luke 5:31–32: It is not the healthy who need a doctor, but the sick. I have not come to call the righteous, but sinners to repentance.

Luke 13:3: Unless you repent, you too will all perish.

Luke 15:3–7: Then Jesus told them this parable: "Suppose one of you has a hundred sheep and loses one of them. Does he not leave the ninety-nine in the open country and go after the lost sheep until he finds it? And when he finds it, he joyfully puts it on his shoulders and goes home. Then he calls his friends and neighbors together and says, 'Rejoice with me; I have found my lost sheep.' I tell you that in the same way there will be more rejoicing in heaven over one sinner who repents than over ninety-nine righteous persons who do not need to repent."

Luke 15:10: There is rejoicing in the presence of the angels of God over one sinner who repents.

Luke 15:17–20: When he came to his senses, he said, "How many of my father's hired men have food to spare, and here I am starving to death! I will set out and go back to my father and say to him: Father, I have sinned against heaven and against you. I am no longer worthy to be called your son; make me like one of your hired men." So he got up and went to his father. But while he was still a long way off, his father saw him and was filled with compassion for him; he ran to his son, threw his arms around him and kissed him.

## Promises

Luke 24:46–47: The Christ will suffer and rise from the dead on the third day, and repentance and forgiveness of sins will be preached in his name to all nations, beginning at Jerusalem.

## Commands

Matthew 4:17: Repent, for the kingdom of heaven is near.

Matthew 23:26: First clean the inside of the cup and dish, and then the outside also will be clean.

Mark 1:15: The Kingdom of God is near. Repent and believe the good news!

## Reflections

*Repentance* is both sorrow for sin and a turning to God. Healthy people do not need a doctor, but when it comes to sin, no one is healthy. All have sinned and come short of the glory of God. Therefore, we all need a doctor—we all need a Savior. And we all need to repent—to turn away from sin and toward righteousness. God in His grace gives us the desire and the power to repent, and we are to respond to God's grace. Turning from sin to righteousness begins by changing the mind and setting the will. The will, then, governs the actions.

Finally, the Holy Spirit will help the body to practice the new behaviors until they become habit. This process constitutes the ongoing sanctification which should take place in Christians throughout their lives (read Psalm 51).

# REST

## Principles

Mark 6:31: Because so many people were coming and going that they did not even have a chance to eat, he said to them, "Come with me by yourselves to a quiet place and get some rest."

## Promises

Matthew 11:28–30: Come to me, all you who are weary and burdened, and I will give you rest. Take my yoke upon you and learn from me, for I am gentle and humble in heart, and you will find rest for your souls. For my yoke is easy and my burden is light.

John 16:33: I have told you these things, so that in me you may have peace. In this world you will have trouble. But take heart! I have overcome the world.

## Reflections

When we work hard we get tired, and it's okay to rest one's body and mind. But real rest is found only in the person of Jesus Christ. Although the body can suffer from fatigue, the greatest tiredness comes from a troubled soul. But Jesus offers rest even while we carry our burdens.

The yoke is designed so that a person can carry a heavy load by balancing it. To find rest, I must take His yoke upon me, meaning I must submit to His will for me. Then I am to assume only the burdens He gives, carrying them only in the way He did, learning how He handled His burdens.

Jesus carried the heaviest load ever, but He responded to it with gentleness and humility. When I submit to Jesus, bear the burdens he wants me to carry, and respond to them the way He did, my soul will be at rest (read Hebrews 4).

# REVELATION

## Principles

Mark 4:22: Whatever is hidden is meant to be disclosed, and whatever is concealed is meant to be brought out into the open.

John 1:1: In the beginning was the Word, and the Word was with God, and the Word was God.

John 1:14: The Word became flesh and made his dwelling among us. We have seen his glory, the glory of the One and Only, who came from the Father, full of grace and truth.

John 1:18: No one has ever seen God, but God the One and Only, who is at the Father's side, has made him known.

John 14:9: Anyone who has seen me has seen the Father. How can you say, "Show us the Father"?

## Promises

John 14:21: Whoever has my commands and obeys them, he is the one who loves me. He who loves me will be loved by my Father, and I too will love him and show myself to him.

John 15:15: I no longer call you servants, because a servant does not know his master's business. Instead, I have called you friends, for everything that I learned from my Father I have made known to you.

## Reflections

*Revelation* is God's disclosure of Himself and His truth, and God reveals Himself to those who love Him. When one loves Jesus, that means a person is loved by God the Father, which opens up the way for true revelation—that Jesus and God are one. Too, loving Jesus means being His friend, and Jesus tells His friends those secrets only He and His Father know.

The key, then, to revelation is love. And this is true on a human level—we reveal ourselves to those who love us (read Revelation 1).

# REWARDS

## *Principles*

Matthew 25:34: The King will say to those on his right, "Come, you who are blessed by my Father; take your inheritance, the kingdom prepared for you since the creation of the world."

## *Promises*

Matthew 5:11–12: Blessed are you when people insult you, persecute you and falsely say all kinds of evil against you because of me. Rejoice and be glad, because great is your reward in heaven, for in the same way they persecuted the prophets who were before you.

Matthew 10:42: If anyone gives even a cup of cold water to one of these little ones because he is my disciple, I tell you the truth, he will certainly not lose his reward.

Matthew 16:27: The Son of Man is going to come in his Father's glory with his angels, and then he will reward each person according to what he has done.

Mark 10:29–30: No one who has left home or brothers or sisters or mother or father or children or fields for me and the gospel will fail to receive a hundred times as much in this present age (homes, brothers, sisters, mothers, children and fields—and with them, persecutions) and in the age to come, eternal life.

Luke 14:12–14: When you give a luncheon or dinner, do not invite your friends, your brothers or relatives, or your rich neighbors; if you do, they may invite you back and so you will be repaid. But when you give a banquet, invite the poor, the crippled, the lame, the blind, and you will be blessed. Although they cannot repay you, you will be repaid at the resurrection of the righteous.

## Commands

Matthew 6:1–6: Be careful not to do your "acts of righteousness" before men, to be seen by them. If you do, you will have no reward from your Father in heaven. So when you give to the needy, do not announce it with trumpets, as the hypocrites do in the synagogues and on the streets, to be honored by men. I tell you the truth, they have received their reward in full. But when you give to the needy, do not let your left hand know what your right hand is doing, so that your giving may be in secret. Then your Father, who sees what is done in secret, will reward you. And when you pray, do not be like the hypocrites, for they love to pray standing in the synagogues and on the street corners to be seen by men. I tell you the truth, they have received their reward in full. But when you pray, go into your room, close the door and pray to your Father, who is unseen. Then your Father, who sees what is done in secret, will reward you.

Matthew 6:16–18: When you fast, do not look somber as the hypocrites do, for they disfigure their faces to show men they are fasting. I tell you the truth, they have received their reward in full. But when you fast, put oil on your head and wash your face, so that it will not be obvious to men that you are fasting, but only to your Father, who is unseen; and your Father, who sees what is done in secret, will reward you.

## Reflections

*Reward* means what God has in store for humans. If our only goal is to receive rewards in this life, then we may well be rewarded here, but not in heaven. The rewards we receive in heaven are given to us by the Father, because we have done something in this life purely for His sake. But God in His amazing grace will often reward us in both heaven and in this life.

# RIGHTEOUSNESS

## Principles

Matthew 5:20: Unless your righteousness surpasses that of the Pharisees and the teachers of the law, you will certainly not enter the kingdom of heaven.

Matthew 25:37–40, 46: Then the righteous will answer him, "Lord, when did we see you hungry and feed you, or thirsty and give you something to drink? When did we see you a stranger and invite you in, or needing clothes and clothe you? When did we see you sick or in prison and go to visit you?" The King will reply, "I tell you the truth, whatever you did for one of the least of these brothers of mine, you did for me." . . . Then [the unrighteous] will go away to eternal punishment, but the righteous to eternal life.

Mark 2:17: It is not the healthy who need a doctor, but the sick. I have not come to call the righteous, but sinners.

## Promises

Matthew 5:6: Blessed are those who hunger and thirst for righteousness, for they will be filled.

## Commands

Matthew 6:33: Seek first his kingdom and his righteousness, and all these things will be given to you as well.

## Reflections

*Righteousness* is the state of being perfect and without sin. I am not righteous in myself nor will I ever become practically righteous on earth. Rather, righteousness is a gift from God, imputed to me through Christ's atonement. I am, nonetheless, to strongly desire to be righteous in practice, knowing that help comes from the Holy Spirit to do so.

The righteousness that I desire must be true righteousness, not self-righteousness. True righteousness is given to me by the Lord Jesus Christ. Righteousness is progressive, however, attained from seeking the things of God first and from knowing and obeying His commands.

# SABBATH

## *Principles*

Matthew 12:8: The Son of Man is Lord of the Sabbath.

Matthew 12:12: It is lawful to do good on the Sabbath.

Mark 2:27: The Sabbath was made for man, not man for the Sabbath.

Luke 13:10, 14–16: On a Sabbath Jesus was teaching in one of the synagogues. . . . Indignant because Jesus had healed on the Sabbath, the synagogue ruler said to the people, "There are six days for work. So come and be healed on those days, not on the Sabbath." The Lord answered him, "You hypocrites! Doesn't each of you on the Sabbath untie his ox or donkey from the stall and lead it out to give it water? Then should not this woman, a daughter of Abraham, whom Satan has kept bound for eighteen long years, be set free on the Sabbath day from what bound her?"

Luke 14:3–5: Jesus asked the Pharisees and experts in the law, "Is it lawful to heal on the Sabbath or not?" But they remained silent. So taking hold of the man, he healed him and sent him away. Then he asked them, "If one of you has a son or an ox that falls into a well on the Sabbath day, will you not immediately pull him out?"

John 5:16–17: Because Jesus was doing these things on the Sabbath, the Jews persecuted him. Jesus said to them, "My Father is always at his work to this very day, and I, too, am working."

## Reflections

The Sabbath—the seventh day of the week—is the day of rest, and is God's gift to me. Jesus is Lord of the Sabbath, and He can do what He pleases with it. I'm not bound by human laws regarding the Sabbath but can do as I am led by God, especially to do good. The Father works to do good to His people, as does Jesus, and I am led by His example.

# SATAN

## *Principles*

Matthew 6:13: Lead us not into temptation, but deliver us from the evil one.

Matthew 12:29: How can anyone enter a strong man's house and carry off his possessions unless he first ties up the strong man? Then he can rob his house.

Matthew 12:43–45: When an evil spirit comes out of a man, it goes through arid places seeking rest and does not find it. Then it says, "I will return to the house I left." When it arrives, it finds the house unoccupied, swept clean and put in order. Then it goes and takes with it seven other spirits more wicked than itself, and they go in and live there. And the final condition of that man is worse than the first. That is how it will be with this wicked generation.

Matthew 13:19: When anyone hears the message about the kingdom and does not understand it, the evil one comes and snatches away what was sown in his heart.

Matthew 16:23: Jesus turned and said to Peter, "Get behind me, Satan! You are a stumbling block to me; you do not have in mind the things of God, but the things of men."

Matthew 25:41: Depart from me, you who are cursed, into the eternal fire prepared for the devil and his angels.

Luke 13:16: Should not this woman, a daughter of Abraham, whom Satan has kept bound for eighteen long years, be set free on the Sabbath day from what bound her?

John 8:44: You belong to your father, the devil, and you want to carry out your father's desire. He was a murderer from the beginning, not holding to the truth, for there is no truth in him. When he lies, he speaks his native language, for he is a liar and the father of lies.

John 14:30: I will not speak with you much longer, for the prince of this world is coming. He has no hold on me.

## *Promises*

Matthew 12:25–26: Every kingdom divided against itself will be ruined, and every city or household divided against itself will not stand. If Satan drives out Satan, he is divided against himself. How then can his kingdom stand?

Luke 11:20: If I drive out demons by the finger of God, then the Kingdom of God has come to you.

Luke 22:31–32: Simon, Simon, Satan has asked to sift you as wheat. But I have prayed for you, Simon, that your faith may not fail. And when you have turned back, strengthen your brothers.

John 12:31–32: Now is the time for judgment on this world; now the prince of this world will be driven out. But I, when I am lifted up from the earth, will draw all men to myself.

## Reflections

Satan is an angel who became the archenemy of God. As such, Satan must be controlled in a person's life before the person can become more godly. But only God can control Satan. I cannot expel Satan from my life, or from the lives of others, but God will do so in answer to my prayer in faith.

When Satan has been expelled, however, something else must take his place or he will return; nature abhors a vacuum. And I, too, when I have been cleansed from sin, must fill my mind with thoughts of God and others so that I will not become trapped again in the sin that was forgiven. And Satan wants me to become trapped, so he lies and his followers lie also.

Any time I think along human lines instead of godly lines, my mind is being controlled by Satan. Thus, I must not use human reasoning alone but discern what Scripture says and then obey God.

# SATISFACTION

## Principles

Matthew 25:34: Come, you who are blessed by my Father; take your inheritance, the kingdom prepared for you since the creation of the world.

Luke 4:4: Man does not live on bread alone.

Luke 6:48: He is like a man building a house, who dug down deep and laid the foundation on rock. When a flood came, the torrent struck that house but could not shake it, because it was well built.

John 4:34: My food . . . is to do the will of him who sent me and to finish his work.

## Promises

Luke 6:21: Blessed are you who hunger now, for you will be satisfied.

John 14:1–3: Do not let your hearts be troubled. Trust in God; trust also in me. In my Father's house are many rooms; if it were not so, I would have told you. I am going there to prepare a place for you. And if I go and prepare a place for you, I will come back and take you to be with me that you also may be where I am.

## Reflections

Satisfaction comes from being filled with the Lord Jesus Christ and from doing His will. When I experience dissatisfaction, then, I must consider whether or not any area of my life is not in the will of God.

The grace of God often comes by His giving me a hunger for Him, creating an aching void inside that can be satisfied only by Him. I am blessed by that grace because the Lord Himself will fill me with His Spirit. When I'm filled with the Spirit, I'm in the will of God, wanting to do His work. This filling of the hunger for God gives me deep satisfaction.

# SECOND COMING

## *Principles*

Matthew 24:27: As lightning that comes from the east is visible even in the west, so will be the coming of the Son of Man.

Matthew 24:31: He will send his angels with a loud trumpet call, and they will gather his elect from the four winds, from one end of the heavens to the other.

Matthew 24:36: No one knows about that day or hour, not even the angels in heaven, nor the Son, but only the Father.

Mark 13:10: The gospel must first be preached to all nations.

Mark 14:62: You will see the Son of Man sitting at the right hand of the Mighty One and coming on the clouds of heaven.

Luke 9:26: If anyone is ashamed of me and my words, the Son of Man will be ashamed of him when he comes in his glory and in the glory of the Father and of the holy angels.

Luke 12:35–40: Be dressed ready for service and keep your lamps burning, like men waiting for their master to return from a wedding banquet, so that when he comes and knocks they can immediately open the door for him. It will be good for those servants whose master finds them watching when he comes. I tell you the truth, he will dress himself to serve, will have them recline at the table and will come and wait on them. It will be good for those servants whose master finds them ready, even if he comes in the second or third watch of the night. But understand this: If the owner of the house had known at what hour the thief was coming, he would not have let his house be broken into. You also must be ready, because the Son of Man will come at an hour when you do not expect him.

Luke 17:29–32: But the day Lot left Sodom, fire and sulfur rained down from heaven and destroyed them all. It will be just like this on the day the Son of Man is revealed. On that day no one who is on the roof of his house, with his goods inside, should go down to get them. Likewise, no one in the field should go back for anything. Remember Lot's wife!

Luke 21:10–11: Nation will rise against nation, and kingdom against kingdom. There will be great earthquakes, famines and pestilences in various places, and fearful events and great signs from heaven.

John 5:28–29: Do not be amazed at this, for a time is coming when all who are in their graves will hear his voice and come out—those who have done good will rise to live, and those who have done evil will rise to be condemned.

John 14:3: If I go and prepare a place for you, I will come back and take you to be with me that you also may be where I am.

## *Promises*

Matthew 16:27: The Son of Man is going to come in his Father's glory with his angels, and then he will reward each person according to what he has done.

Matthew 24:30: At that time the sign of the Son of Man will appear in the sky, and all the nations of the earth will mourn. They will see the Son of Man coming on the clouds of the sky, with power and great glory.

Luke 21:27–28: At that time they will see the Son of Man coming in a cloud with power and great glory. When these things begin to take place, stand up and lift up your heads, because your redemption is drawing near.

## *Commands*

Matthew 24:44: You also must be ready, because the Son of Man will come at an hour when you do not expect him.

Mark 13:5–7: Watch out that no one deceives you. Many will come in my name, claiming, "I am he," and will deceive many. When you hear of wars and rumors of wars, do not be alarmed. Such things must happen, but the end is still to come.

Mark 13:32–33: No one knows about that day or hour, not even the angels in heaven, nor the Son, but only the Father. Be on guard! Be alert! You do not know when that time will come.

Mark 13:36–37: If he comes suddenly, do not let him find you sleeping. What I say to you, I say to everyone: "Watch!"

Luke 21:34–36: Be careful, or your hearts will be weighed down with dissipation, drunkenness and the anxieties of life, and that day will close on you unexpectedly like a trap. For it will come upon all those who live on the face of the whole earth. Be always on the watch, and pray that you may be able to escape all that is about to happen, and that you may be able to stand before the Son of Man.

## Reflections

The *Second Coming* means the return of Jesus to judge the world and establish His kingdom on earth. I am to watch for Christ's coming and be ready for it, because it may occur at any time; there will be no further warning. I want to say at any moment of any day, "I am ready." And in the meantime I'm to be busy about the Lord's work. Because Christ may not return in my natural lifetime, I don't want to waste any time that God has given me on earth.

# SELF-DENIAL

## *Principles*

Mark 10:42–44: Those who are regarded as rulers of the Gentiles lord it over them, and their high officials exercise authority over them. Not so with you. Instead, whoever wants to become great among you must be your servant, and whoever wants to be first must be slave of all.

Luke 6:25: Woe to you who are well fed now, for you will go hungry. Woe to you who laugh now, for you will mourn and weep.

Luke 12:20–21: God said to him, "You fool! This very night your life will be demanded from you. Then who will get what you have prepared for yourself?" This is how it will be with anyone who stores up things for himself but is not rich toward God.

Luke 18:29–30: I tell you the truth, . . . no one who has left home or wife or brothers or parents or children for the sake of the Kingdom of God will fail to receive many times as much in this age and, in the age to come, eternal life.

Luke 22:25–27: The kings of the Gentiles lord it over them; and those who exercise authority over them call themselves Benefactors. But you are not to be like that. Instead, the greatest among you should be like the youngest, and the one who rules like the one who serves. For who is greater, the one who is at the table or the one who serves? Is it not the one who is at the table? But I am among you as one who serves.

## Promises

Matthew 16:25: Whoever wants to save his life will lose it, but whoever loses his life for me will find it.

Mark 8:35: Whoever wants to save his life will lose it, but whoever loses his life for me and for the gospel will save it.

Mark 10:29–30: No one who has left home or brothers or sisters or mother or father or children or fields for me and the gospel will fail to receive a hundred times as much in this present age (homes, brothers, sisters, mothers, children and fields—and with them, persecutions) and in the age to come, eternal life.

John 12:24–26: Unless a kernel of wheat falls to the ground and dies, it remains only a single seed. But if it dies, it produces many seeds. The man who loves his life will lose it, while the man who hates his life in this world will keep it for eternal life. Whoever serves me, must follow me; and where I am, my servant also will be. My Father will honor the one who serves me.

## Commands

Matthew 5:29–30: If your right eye causes you to sin, gouge it out and throw it away. It is better for you to lose one part of your body than for your whole body to be thrown into hell. And if your right hand causes you to sin, cut it off and throw it away. It is better for you to lose one part of your body than for your whole body to go into hell.

Matthew 5:39–42: Do not resist an evil person. If someone strikes you on the right cheek, turn to him the other also. And if someone wants to sue you and take your tunic, let him have your cloak as well. If someone forces you to go one mile, go with him two miles. Give to the one who asks you, and do not turn away from the one who wants to borrow from you.

Matthew 10:37–39: Anyone who loves his father or mother more than me is not worthy of me; anyone who loves his son or daughter more than me is not worthy of me; and anyone who does not take his cross and follow me is not worthy of me. Whoever finds his life will lose it, and whoever loses his life for my sake will find it.

Luke 9:23–25: If anyone would come after me, he must deny himself and take up his cross daily and follow me. For whoever wants to save his life will lose it, but whoever loses his life for me will save it. What good is it for a man to gain the whole world, and yet lose or forfeit his very self?

Luke 14:26–33: If anyone comes to me and does not hate his father and mother, his wife and children, his brothers and sisters—yes, even his own life—he cannot be my disciple. And anyone who does not carry his cross and follow me cannot be my disciple. Suppose one of you wants to build a tower. Will he not first sit down and estimate the cost to see if he has enough money to complete it? For if he lays the foundation and is not able to finish it, everyone who sees it will ridicule him, saying, "This fellow began to build and was not able to finish." Or suppose a king is about to go to war against another king. Will he not first sit down and consider whether he is able with ten thousand men to oppose the one coming against him with twenty thousand? If he is not able, he will send a delegation while the other is still a long way off and will ask for terms of peace. In the same way, any of you who does not give up everything he has cannot be my disciple.

## Reflections

It's difficult not to be self-centered; self-denial doesn't come naturally. It's human nature to always think of self first, last, and in between. The Holy Spirit prompts us to give of ourselves to God, but it takes His power—coupled with our will—to effect it. True, through self-discipline it's possible to deny ourselves in one or two areas of life. But without the Holy Spirit this denial quickly becomes asceticism and will not prevail in all areas of life.

Yet to deny the self is what we're commanded to do. It's practical in the long run, and many wonderful promises are related to it. But without the life of Christ in us we cannot accomplish it. Self-denial becomes the desire of the child of God, and God uses our inability to deny ourselves in order to keep us dependent upon Him.

# SERVICE

## *Principles*

Mark 9:35: If anyone wants to be first, he must be the very last, and the servant of all.

Mark 10:43–45: Whoever wants to become great among you must be your servant, and whoever wants to be first must be slave of all. For even the Son of Man did not come to be served, but to serve, and to give his life as a ransom for many.

Luke 16:13: No servant can serve two masters. Either he will hate the one and love the other, or he will be devoted to the one and despise the other. You cannot serve both God and Money.

Luke 17:10: When you have done everything you were told to do, should say, "We are unworthy servants; we have only done our duty."

## *Promises*

Matthew 25:40: Whatever you did for one of the least of these brothers of mine, you did for me.

## *Commands*

Luke 4:8: Worship the Lord your God and serve him only.

John 13:13–17: You call me "Teacher" and "Lord," and rightly so, for that is what I am. Now that I, your Lord and Teacher, have washed your feet, you also should wash one another's feet. I have set you an example that you should do as I have done for you. I tell you the truth, no servant is greater than his master, nor is a messenger greater than the one who sent him. Now that you know these things, you will be blessed if you do them.

## Reflections

Jesus never claimed that service was to be fulfilling for the servant. If, as a servant, I'm concerned with my fulfillment then I'm, in fact, serving two masters—others and myself. That won't work. To serve means to become a servant of Christ—to do what He asks for the benefit of others. When we serve with the right motive, then we find that God in His grace makes us feel fulfilled.

# SIGHT

## Principles

John 20:29: Because you have seen me, you have believed; blessed are those who have not seen and yet have believed.

## Promises

Luke 8:10: The knowledge of the secrets of the Kingdom of God has been given to you, but to others I speak in parables, so that, "though seeing, they may not see; though hearing, they may not understand."

John 1:39: Come, . . . and you will see.

John 1:50: You believe because I told you I saw you under the fig tree. You shall see greater things than that.

John 9:39: For judgment I have come into this world, so that the blind will see and those who see will become blind.

## Reflections

*Seeing* can mean either observing with the eyes or understanding with the mind. Neither demands faith. But to believe what you don't observe or what you don't understand requires faith. Jesus wants me to believe His words even when I don't see the evidence of their truth or understand their meaning. After I believe, He will let me see the things that confirm my belief, showing me what has been there all along.

# SINGLE-MINDEDNESS

## Principles

Matthew 6:22: The eye is the lamp of the body. If your eyes are good, your whole body will be full of light.

Matthew 6:24: No one can serve two masters. Either he will hate the one and love the other, or he will be devoted to the one and despise the other. You cannot serve both God and Money.

## Promises

Luke 12:31: Seek his kingdom, and these things will be given to you as well.

## Commands

Matthew 4:10: Away from me, Satan! For it is written: "Worship the Lord your God, and serve him only."

Mark 12:30: Love the Lord your God with all your heart and with all your soul and with all your mind and with all your strength.

## Reflections

*Single-mindedness* doesn't mean that I have no priorities; it means that I can't do two things at the same time. I must make a choice.

- I cannot look after myself and the things of the Lord at the same time.
- I cannot look in two directions at the same time.
- I cannot serve two masters at the same time.
- If I want to be Christlike, I cannot be worldly.
- If I want to be a giving person, I cannot keep everything for myself.
- If I want to be loving, I cannot hate anyone.
- If I want to be humble, I cannot be proud of myself.

# SOVEREIGNTY

## Principles

Matthew 20:15–16: Don't I have the right to do what I want with my own money? Or are you envious because I am generous? So the last will be first, and the first will be last.

Matthew 22:14: For many are invited, but few are chosen.

## Promises

John 15:16: You did not choose me, but I chose you and appointed you to go and bear fruit—fruit that will last. Then the Father will give you whatever you ask in my name.

Acts 1:7–8: It is not for you to know the times or dates the Father has set by his own authority. But you will receive power when the Holy Spirit comes on you; and you will be my witnesses in Jerusalem, and in all Judea and Samaria, and to the ends of the earth.

## Reflections

Jesus doesn't give me any commands or any promises in regard to sovereignty, because sovereignty is His domain. The implicit command is to accept His sovereignty without complaint. If I do, He promises that I will bear fruit for Him for eternity—fruit that will be manifest in my own life and in the lives of others.

# STEWARDSHIP

Matthew 6:25–34: Do not worry about your life, what you will eat or drink; or about your body, what you will wear. Is not life more important than food, and the body more important than clothes? Look at the birds of the air; they do not sow or reap or store away in barns, and yet your heavenly Father feeds them. Are you not much more valuable than they? Who of you by worrying can add a single hour to his life? And why do you worry about clothes? See how the lilies of the field grow. They do not labor or spin. Yet I tell you that not even Solomon in all his splendor was dressed like one of these. If that is how God clothes the grass of the field, which is here today and tomorrow is thrown into the fire, will he not much more clothe you, O you of little faith? So do not worry, saying, "What shall we eat?" or "What shall we drink?" or "What shall we wear?" For the pagans run after all these things, and your heavenly Father knows that you need them. But seek first his kingdom and his righteousness, and all these things will be given to you as well. Therefore do not worry about tomorrow, for tomorrow will worry about itself. Each day has enough trouble of its own.

Matthew 19:21: If you want to be perfect, go, sell your possessions and give to the poor, and you will have treasure in heaven. Then come, follow me.

Matthew 25:14–27: [The kingdom of heaven] will be like a man going on a journey, who called his servants and entrusted his property to them. To one he gave five talents of money, to another two talents, and to another one talent, each according to his ability. Then he went on his journey. The man who had received the five talents went at once and put his money to work and gained five more. So also, the one with the two talents gained two more. But the man who had received the one talent went off, dug a hole in the ground and hid his master's money. After a long time the master of those servants returned and settled accounts with them. The man who had received the five talents brought the other five. "Master," he said, "you entrusted me with five talents. See, I have gained five more." His master replied, "Well done, good and faithful servant! You have been faithful with a few things; I will put you in charge of many things. Come and share your master's happiness!" The man with the two talents also came. "Master," he said, "you entrusted me with two talents; see, I have gained two more." His master replied, "Well done, good and faithful servant! You have been faithful with a few things; I will put you in charge of many things. Come and share your master's happiness!" Then the man who had received the one talent came. "Master," he said, "I knew that you are a hard man, harvesting where you have not sown and gathering where you have not scattered seed. So I was afraid and went out and hid your talent in the ground. See, here is what belongs to you." His master replied, "You wicked, lazy servant! So you knew that I harvest where I have not sown and gather where I have not scattered seed? Well then, you should have put my money on deposit with the bankers, so that when I returned I would have received it back with interest."

Luke 19:26: I tell you that to everyone who has, more will be given, but as for the one who has nothing, even what he has will be taken away.

## *Promises*

Matthew 10:32: Whoever acknowledges me before men, I will also acknowledge him before my Father in heaven.

Luke 16:10–12: Whoever can be trusted with very little can also be trusted with much, and whoever is dishonest with very little will also be dishonest with much. So if you have not been trustworthy in handling worldly wealth, who will trust you with true riches? And if you have not been trustworthy with someone else's property, who will give you property of your own?

## *Commands*

Luke 16:9: Use worldly wealth to gain friends for yourselves, so that when it is gone, you will be welcomed into eternal dwellings.

## *Reflections*

*Stewardship* is how one handles what God has given; worldly goods as well as spiritual treasures. My handling of worldly wealth, especially that belonging to someone else, is an indication of my trustworthiness in society. But since all things belong to God, how I handle all things is an indication of my relationship with Him.

# STUMBLING

## Principles

Matthew 16:22–23: Peter took him aside and began to rebuke him. "Never, Lord!" he said. "This shall never happen to you!" Jesus turned and said to Peter, "Get behind me, Satan! You are a stumbling block to me; you do not have in mind the things of God, but the things of men."

John 11:9–10: Are there not twelve hours of daylight? A man who walks by day will not stumble, for he sees by this world's light. It is when he walks by night that he stumbles, for he has no light.

## Commands

Luke 17:1–3: Things that cause people to sin are bound to come, but woe to that person through whom they come. It would be better for him to be thrown into the sea with a millstone tied around his neck than for him to cause one of these little ones to sin. So watch yourselves. If your brother sins, rebuke him, and if he repents, forgive him.

## Reflections

Certainly we can stumble ourselves, but woe to the person who causes another to stumble. Woe to me if I give wrong advice, set a bad example, direct others to do something not pleasing to God, manipulate others for my own use. I myself stumble when I sin, and I sin when I either don't or won't see the things of God but only the things of the world.

# SUBMISSION

## Principles

Matthew 21:44: He who falls on this stone will be broken to pieces, but he on whom it falls will be crushed.

Matthew 26:39: My Father, if it is possible, may this cup be taken from me. Yet not as I will, but as you will.

Luke 14:27: Anyone who does not carry his cross and follow me cannot be my disciple.

## Promises

Matthew 10:39: Whoever finds his life will lose it, and whoever loses his life for my sake will find it.

Matthew 11:29–30: Take my yoke upon you and learn from me, for I am gentle and humble in heart, and you will find rest for your souls. For my yoke is easy and my burden is light.

## Commands

John 2:5: Do whatever he tells you.

## Reflections

*Submission* means giving in to the will of another, and we may submit willingly or unwillingly. Jesus always willingly submitted to His Father's will. Submission to God's will, then, is the mark of a Christian. Moreover, when we willingly submit to the Lord, we experience rest to our souls.

## T

# TEMPTATION

## *Principles*

Matthew 4:1–11: Jesus was led by the Spirit into the desert to be tempted by the devil. After fasting forty days and forty nights, he was hungry. The tempter came to him and said, "If you are the Son of God, tell these stones to become bread." Jesus answered, "It is written: 'Man does not live on bread alone, but on every word that comes from the mouth of God.'" Then the devil took him to the holy city and had him stand on the highest point of the temple. "If you are the Son of God," he said, "throw yourself down. For it is written: 'He will command his angels concerning you, and they will lift you up in their hands, so that you will not strike your foot against a stone.'" Jesus answered him, "It is also written: 'Do not put the Lord your God to the test.'" Again, the devil took him to a very high mountain and showed him all the kingdoms of the world and their splendor. "All this I will give you," he said, "if you will bow down and worship me." Jesus said to him, "Away from me, Satan! For it is written: 'Worship the Lord your God, and serve him only.'" Then the devil left him, and angels came and attended him.

Matthew 5:29–30: If your right eye causes you to sin, gouge it out and throw it away. It is better for you to lose one part of your body than for your whole body to be thrown into hell. And if your right hand causes you to sin, cut it off and throw it away. It is better for you to lose one part of your body than for your whole body to go into hell.

Matthew 7:13–14: Enter through the narrow gate. For wide is the gate and broad is the road that leads to destruction, and many enter through it. But small is the gate and narrow the road that leads to life, and only a few find it.

Matthew 18:7–9: Woe to the world because of the things that cause people to sin! Such things must come, but woe to the man through whom they come! If your hand or your foot causes you to sin, cut it off and throw it away. It is better for you to enter life maimed or crippled than to have two hands or two feet and be thrown into eternal fire. And if your eye causes you to sin, gouge it out and throw it away. It is better for you to enter life with one eye than to have two eyes and be thrown into the fire of hell.

## Promises

Matthew 6:13: Lead us not into temptation, but deliver us from the evil one.

## Commands

Matthew 26:41: Watch and pray so that you will not fall into temptation. The spirit is willing, but the body is weak.

Luke 22:40: Pray that you will not fall into temptation.

Luke 22:46: Why are you sleeping? . . . Get up and pray so that you will not fall into temptation.

## *Reflections*

    *Temptation* means enticing one to sin against God. The Devil tempts us, using the world, other people, and our own flesh to do so. And he often uses us to tempt others. The way we avoid temptation is by prayer and the use of Scripture. Jesus uses the phrase "fall into temptation," which has the meaning of giving in to it. Temptations hinder our effectiveness for God, and they are bound to come. But we needn't give in to them. We are to be careful—we are to watch—and we are to pray so that we will not fall into temptation.

# TRADITION

## *Principles*

Mark 7:6–13: Isaiah was right when he prophesied about you hypocrites; as it is written: "These people honor me with their lips, but their hearts are far from me. They worship me in vain; their teachings are but rules taught by men." You have let go of the commands of God and are holding on to the traditions of men. . . . You have a fine way of setting aside the commands of God in order to observe your own traditions! For Moses said, "Honor your father and your mother," and, "Anyone who curses his father or mother must be put to death." But you say that if a man says to his father or mother: Whatever help you might otherwise have received from me is Corban" (that is, a gift devoted to God), then you no longer let him do anything for his father or mother. Thus you nullify the word of God by your tradition that you have handed down. And you do many things like that.

Luke 5:36–38: No one tears a patch from a new garment and sews it on an old one. If he does, he will have torn the new garment, and the patch from the new will not match the old. And no one pours new wine into old wineskins. If he does, the new wine will burst the skins, the wine will run out and the wineskins will be ruined. No, new wine must be poured into new wineskins.

# Reflections

Traditions are teachings and religious observances that have been handed down from one generation of people to the next. There's nothing wrong with traditions—as long as they're used properly. No commands and no promises are given when it comes to putting the new life in Christ into the old patterns of living—because it can't be done. Nor do traditions nullify the commands of God. God's will always comes before traditions.

# TRUTH

## *Principles*

John 1:14: The Word became flesh and made his dwelling among us. We have seen his glory, the glory of the One and Only, who came from the Father, full of grace and truth.

John 4:23–24: A time is coming and has now come when the true worshipers will worship the Father in spirit and truth, for they are the kind of worshipers the Father seeks. God is spirit, and his worshipers must worship in spirit and in truth.

John 8:45–46: Because I tell the truth, you do not believe me! Can any of you prove me guilty of sin? If I am telling the truth, why don't you believe me?

John 14:6: I am the way and the truth and the life. No one comes to the Father except through me.

John 14:17–18: [The Father will give you] the Spirit of truth. The world cannot accept him, because it neither sees him nor knows him. But you know him, for he lives with you and will be in you. I will not leave you as orphans; I will come to you.

John 16:13: When he, the Spirit of truth, comes, he will guide you into all truth. He will not speak on his own; he will speak only what he hears, and he will tell you what is yet to come.

John 17:17: Sanctify them by the truth; your word is truth.

John 18:37: You are right in saying I am a king. In fact, for this reason I was born, and for this I came into the world, to testify to the truth. Everyone on the side of truth listens to me.

## Promises

John 3:21: Whoever lives by the truth comes into the light, so that it may be seen plainly that what he has done has been done through God.

John 8:31–32: If you hold to my teaching, you are really my disciples. Then you will know the truth, and the truth will set you free.

## Reflections

Truth is that which is accurate and agrees with reality, and truth characterizes God the Father, Son, and Holy Spirit. Truth also characterizes God's Word. I must know it, seek it, choose it, buy it, believe it, love it, walk in it, live by it, obey it, worship in it, and speak it. And if I do so, what does truth do for me? It protects me, guides me, sets me free, sanctifies and purifies me.

# U

# UNITY

## Principles

John 10:16: I have other sheep that are not of this sheep pen. I must bring them also. They too will listen to my voice, and there shall be one flock and one shepherd.

John 17:21–23: [My prayer is] that all of them may be one, Father, just as you are in me and I am in you. May they also be in us so that the world may believe that you have sent me. I have given them the glory that you gave me, that they may be one as we are one: I in them and you in me. May they be brought to complete unity to let the world know that you sent me and have loved them even as you have loved me.

## Reflections

Only when Christ resides in each person can the possibility of complete unity exist among people. Although Christians and non-Christians may cooperate with each other, they can never experience complete unity—because unity connotes agreement in purpose. Believers and nonbelievers can have common goals, but their purpose in achieving those goals is different. A Christian's purpose for every goal is to glorify God.

# V

# VALUES

## Principles

Matthew 6:25: Do not worry about your life, what you will eat or drink; or about your body, what you will wear. Is not life more important than food, and the body more important than clothes?

Mark 8:36: What good is it for a man to gain the whole world, yet forfeit his soul?

Luke 16:15: You are the ones who justify yourselves in the eyes of men, but God knows your hearts. What is highly valued among men is detestable in God's sight.

## Commands

John 6:27: Do not work for food that spoils, but for food that endures to eternal life, which the Son of Man will give you. On him God the Father has placed his seal of approval.

## Reflections

Values are different from priorities: values relate to the heart while priorities relate to actions. At times our first priority is to fix food or make clothes, because we must eat and have something to wear. Great value should not be placed on these things, however, except as they sustain life.

The things we must do, therefore, should not direct our hearts even though they often direct our actions. In practice, then, if preparing food or clothing causes me to become anxious, or covetous, or selfish, then they are affecting my heart. I must confess as much to God and surrender my care over those chores to Him.

# W

# WEALTH

## *Principles*

Matthew 6:24–25: No one can serve two masters. Either he will hate the one and love the other, or he will be devoted to the one and despise the other. You cannot serve both God and Money. Therefore I tell you, do not worry about your life, what you will eat or drink; or about your body, what you will wear. Is not life more important than food, and the body more important than clothes?

Matthew 13:22: The one who received the seed that fell among the thorns is the man who hears the word, but the worries of this life and the deceitfulness of wealth choke it, making it unfruitful.

Matthew 22:21: Give to Caesar what is Caesar's, and to God what is God's.

Luke 6:24: Woe to you who are rich, for you have already received your comfort.

Luke 12:34: Where your treasure is, there your heart will be also.

Luke 18:24–25: How hard it is for the rich to enter the Kingdom of God! Indeed, it is easier for a camel to go through the eye of a needle than for a rich man to enter the Kingdom of God.

## Promises

Matthew 6:20–21: Store up for yourselves treasures in heaven, where moth and rust do not destroy, and where thieves do not break in and steal. For where your treasure is, there your heart will be also.

Matthew 6:33: Seek first his kingdom and his righteousness, and all these things will be given to you as well.

## Commands

Matthew 6:19–21: Do not store up for yourselves treasures on earth, where moth and rust destroy, and where thieves break in and steal. But store up for yourselves treasures in heaven, where moth and rust do not destroy, and where thieves do not break in and steal. For where your treasure is, there your heart will be also.

Matthew 6:25: Do not worry about your life, what you will eat or drink; or about your body, what you will wear. Is not life more important than food, and the body more important than clothes?

Matthew 19:21: If you want to be perfect, go, sell your possessions and give to the poor, and you will have treasure in heaven. Then come, follow me.

Luke 12:15: Watch out! Be on your guard against all kinds of greed; a man's life does not consist in the abundance of his possessions.

Luke 12:33: Sell your possessions and give to the poor. Provide purses for yourselves that will not wear out, a treasure in heaven that will not be exhausted, where no thief comes near and no moth destroys.

## Reflections

Since Jesus will take care of our needs, we need not concentrate on becoming wealthy. A focus on becoming wealthy is, in fact, a great danger; not only can it distract from more important things, it can ruin a person's life. Our focus should be on the things of God, on being holy, on investing our lives in those things which are eternal—namely human souls.

# WISDOM

## *Principles*

Matthew 7:24–26: Everyone who hears these words of mine and puts them into practice is like a wise man who built his house on the rock. The rain came down, the streams rose, and the winds blew and beat against that house; yet it did not fall, because it had its foundation on the rock. But everyone who hears these words of mine and does not put them into practice is like a foolish man who built his house on sand.

Matthew 11:19: Wisdom is proved right by her actions.

Matthew 25:1–13: At that time the kingdom of heaven will be like ten virgins who took their lamps and went out to meet the bridegroom. Five of them were foolish and five were wise. The foolish ones took their lamps but did not take any oil with them. The wise, however, took oil in jars along with their lamps. The bridegroom was a long time in coming, and they all became drowsy and fell asleep. At midnight the cry rang out: "Here's the bridegroom! Come out to meet him!" Then all the virgins woke up and trimmed their lamps. The foolish ones said to the wise, "Give us some of your oil; our lamps are going out." "No," they replied, "there may not be enough for both us and you. Instead, go to those who sell oil and buy some for your-selves." But while they were on their way to buy the oil, the bridegroom arrived. The virgins who were ready went in with him to the wedding banquet. And the door was shut.

Later the others also came. "Sir! Sir!" they said. "Open the door for us!" But he replied, "I tell you the truth, I don't know you." Therefore keep watch, because you do not know the day or the hour.

Luke 7:35: Wisdom is proved right by all her children.

## *Promises*

John 14:26: The Counselor, the Holy Spirit, whom the Father will send in my name, will teach you all things and will remind you of everything I have said to you.

## *Reflections*

Jesus doesn't command us to be wise, but other portions of the Bible exhort us to be so. But what is wisdom? It is comprehensive knowledge, put into practice. Wisdom, then, isn't just knowing a lot, it is putting into practice the lot that I know. Thus, when I seek wisdom, I seek to know the things that I should do.

I am not to seek knowledge solely, however, for knowledge's sake, but to put that knowledge into practice. As I do so, my actions prove whether I am wise. Following God's law and preparing for the future, for example, are wise actions. In the end, the results of my life prove whether or not I have been wise.

# WITNESS

## Principles

Matthew 5:13–15: You are the salt of the earth. But if the salt loses its saltiness, how can it be made salty again? It is no longer good for anything, except to be thrown out and trampled by men. You are the light of the world. A city on a hill cannot be hidden. Neither do people light a lamp and put it under a bowl. Instead they put it on its stand, and it gives light to everyone in the house.

Luke 6:44: Each tree is recognized by its own fruit. People do not pick figs from thornbushes, or grapes from briers.

Luke 16:16: The Law and the Prophets were proclaimed until John. Since that time, the good news of the Kingdom of God is being preached, and everyone is forcing his way into it.

## Promises

John 1:7: He came as a witness to testify concerning that light, so that through him all men might believe.

John 5:33–34: You have sent to John and he has testified to the truth. Not that I accept human testimony; but I mention it that you may be saved.

John 8:18: I am one who testifies for myself; my other witness is the Father, who sent me.

John 15:26: When the Counselor comes, whom I will send to you from the Father, the Spirit of truth who goes out from the Father, he will testify about me.

John 18:37: "You are a king, then!" said Pilate. Jesus answered, "You are right in saying I am a king. In fact, for this reason I was born, and for this I came into the world, to testify to the truth. Everyone on the side of truth listens to me."

## Commands

Matthew 5:16: Let your light shine before men, that they may see your good deeds and praise your Father in heaven.

Mark 5:19: Go home to your family and tell them how much the Lord has done for you, and how he has had mercy on you.

Luke 9:60: Let the dead bury their own dead, but you go and proclaim the Kingdom of God.

## Reflections

A *witness* is one who bears testimony to something or someone. Jesus doesn't need my testimony, but I need to testify. And I must take care that the testimony that I live matches my words. My actions, in fact, make people attend to my words. My words, however, should be about Jesus, not about myself. When I speak of Jesus, God in His grace uses my testimony in His saving process of others.

# WORDS

## Principles

Matthew 5:37: Simply let your "Yes" be "Yes," and your "No," "No"; anything beyond this comes from the evil one.

Matthew 12:37: By your words you will be acquitted, and by your words you will be condemned.

Matthew 15:18: The things that come out of the mouth come from the heart, and these make a man "unclean."

Luke 6:45: The good man brings good things out of the good stored up in his heart, and the evil man brings evil things out of the evil stored up in his heart. For out of the overflow of his heart his mouth speaks.

John 12:48: There is a judge for the one who rejects me and does not accept my words; that very word which I spoke will condemn him at the last day.

## Promises

Luke 12:11–12: When you are brought before synagogues, rulers and authorities, do not worry about how you will defend yourselves or what you will say, for the Holy Spirit will teach you at that time what you should say.

## Commands

Matthew 5:33–36: It was said to the people long ago, "Do not break your oath, but keep the oaths you have made to the Lord." But I tell you, Do not swear at all: either by heaven, for it is God's throne; or by the earth, for it is his footstool; or by Jerusalem, for it is the city of the Great King. And do not swear by your head, for you cannot make even one hair white or black.

Luke 6:28: Bless those who curse you, pray for those who mistreat you.

## Reflections

Although my actions affect other people more than my words do, I am nonetheless acquitted or condemned more by my words than by my actions. By my words I acquit or condemn myself, because words reflect what is inside of me, revealing my motives. My actions are hard to prove without several witnesses, but God judges what is inside of me—that is, what is in my heart—and it is out of the heart that the mouth speaks.

Spoken oaths are not necessary for Christians, although Christians do make commitments that are documented by contracts. A signature on a piece of paper means that a Christian has given his or her word. But a Christian's reputation should be so good that his or her word is enough.

# WORK

## *Principles*

Luke 10:7: Stay in that house, eating and drinking whatever they give you, for the worker deserves his wages. Do not move around from house to house.

Luke 12:48: From everyone who has been given much, much will be demanded; and from the one who has been entrusted with much, much more will be asked.

John 4:34: My food . . . is to do the will of him who sent me and to finish his work.

John 5:17: My Father is always at his work to this very day, and I, too, am working.

John 5:19: The Son can do nothing by himself; he can do only what he sees his Father doing, because whatever the Father does the Son also does.

John 6:29: The work of God is this: to believe in the one he has sent.

John 7:18: He who speaks on his own does so to gain honor for himself, but he who works for the honor of the one who sent him is a man of truth; there is nothing false about him.

John 9:4: As long as it is day, we must do the work of him who sent me. Night is coming, when no one can work.

## Promises

John 7:17: If anyone chooses to do God's will, he will find out whether my teaching comes from God or whether I speak on my own.

John 14:12: Anyone who has faith in me will do what I have been doing. He will do even greater things than these, because I am going to the Father.

## Commands

Luke 17:10: When you have done everything you were told to do, should say, "We are unworthy servants; we have only done our duty."

John 6:27: Do not work for food that spoils, but for food that endures to eternal life, which the Son of Man will give you. On him God the Father has placed his seal of approval.

## Reflections

Jesus expects people to be workers, assuming that everyone works for one thing or another. The question is, For what and for whom do people work? As Christians, we are to work for the one who sent us—Jesus Christ. And the kind of work that Jesus gives us is that which endures to eternal life.

Jesus often speaks of rest, and we can have rest in the middle of hard work. But Jesus never speaks of relaxation or vacation. I may relax my body, then, but never my mind or my spirit. Because when I spend too much time relaxing my mind or my spirit, I get into trouble.

# WORLD

## Principles

John 3:19: This is the verdict: Light has come into the world, but men loved darkness instead of light because their deeds were evil.

John 14:30–31: I will not speak with you much longer, for the prince of this world is coming. He has no hold on me, but the world must learn that I love the Father and that I do exactly what my Father has commanded me.

John 17:14–16: I have given them your word and the world has hated them, for they are not of the world any more than I am of the world. My prayer is not that you take them out of the world but that you protect them from the evil one. They are not of the world, even as I am not of it.

John 17:18: As you sent me into the world, I have sent them into the world.

## Promises

Matthew 24:14: This gospel of the kingdom will be preached in the whole world as a testimony to all nations, and then the end will come.

John 3:16–17: For God so loved the world that he gave his one and only Son, that whoever believes in him shall not perish but have eternal life. For God did not send his Son into the world to condemn the world, but to save the world through him.

John 6:33: The bread of God is he who comes down from heaven and gives life to the world.

John 6:51: I am the living bread that came down from heaven. If anyone eats of this bread, he will live forever. This bread is my flesh, which I will give for the life of the world.

John 8:12: I am the light of the world. Whoever follows me will never walk in darkness, but will have the light of life.

John 15:18–21: If the world hates you, keep in mind that it hated me first. If you belonged to the world, it would love you as its own. As it is, you do not belong to the world, but I have chosen you out of the world. That is why the world hates you. Remember the words I spoke to you: "No servant is greater than his master." If they persecuted me, they will persecute you also. If they obeyed my teaching, they will obey yours also. They will treat you this way because of my name, for they do not know the One who sent me.

John 16:33: I have told you these things, so that in me you may have peace. In this world you will have trouble. But take heart! I have overcome the world.

John 17:23: I in them and you in me. May they be brought to complete unity to let the world know that you sent me and have loved them even as you have loved me.

## Commands

Matthew 28:19: Go and make disciples of all nations, baptizing them in the name of the Father and of the Son and of the Holy Spirit.

Mark 16:15: Go into all the world and preach the good news to all creation.

## Reflections

God loved the world so much that He gave His Son, Jesus, to those who would believe. And Jesus came not only to save the world but to shine light in a place of darkness. But people loved darkness because they followed the Devil, the prince of this world.

Believers, however, are no longer of this world. But because we must live in it, we are affected by it. Believers will be hated by the world and will always encounter trouble, but Jesus' prayers for them protect them from the Evil One.

In spite of persecution, Jesus' followers are to go into all the world, preaching the Good News, the gospel of Jesus Christ, to all.

# WORRY

## Principles

Matthew 6:25–27: Look at the birds of the air; they do not sow or reap or store away in barns, and yet your heavenly Father feeds them. Are you not much more valuable than they? Who of you by worrying can add a single hour to his life?

Matthew 6:34: Do not worry about tomorrow, for tomorrow will worry about itself. Each day has enough trouble of its own.

## Promises

Matthew 10:19–20: When they arrest you, do not worry about what to say or how to say it. At that time you will be given what to say, for it will not be you speaking, but the Spirit of your Father speaking through you.

John 14:27: Peace I leave with you; my peace I give you. I do not give to you as the world gives. Do not let your hearts be troubled and do not be afraid.

## Commands

Luke 12:22–23: Do not worry about your life, what you will eat; or about your body, what you will wear. Life is more than food, and the body more than clothes.

Luke 12:29: Do not set your heart on what you will eat or drink; do not worry about it.

John 14:1: Do not let your hearts be troubled. Trust in God; trust also in me.

## Reflections

Jesus says that I am not to worry about what to eat, what to wear, how long I will live, what tomorrow will bring, how I am to defend myself. In other words, stop worrying about myself, stop being self-centered. Jesus promises that when I stop worrying about myself, God will take care of me. Freedom from worry about myself lets me be concerned about others and the work God would have me do.

# WORSHIP

## Principles

John 4:23-24: A time is coming and has now come when the true worshipers will worship the Father in spirit and truth, for they are the kind of worshipers the Father seeks. God is spirit, and his worshipers must worship in spirit and in truth.

## Promises

Matthew 4:10: Jesus said to [the Devil], "Away from me, Satan! For it is written: 'Worship the Lord your God, and serve him only.'"

## Commands

Luke 4:8: Worship the Lord your God and serve him only.

## Reflections

Jesus gives a simple command: Worship the Lord your God. If God is God, then He alone is to be worshiped. Then Jesus tells us how we are to worship—in spirit and in truth. But unless our spirits have been quickened by the Holy Spirit, we cannot worship God. Nor can we worship God unless we are completely sincere. Just mouthing words is not enough; we must believe the words we utter. Finally, worship drives Satan away, because he cannot function where there is true worship. What a comforting thought!

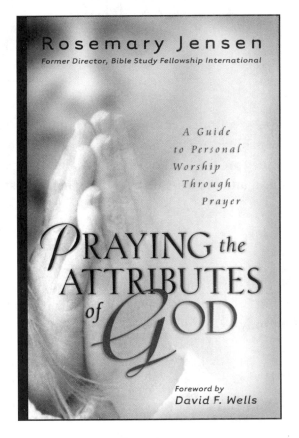

## Praying the Attributes of God
*A Guide to Personal Worship Through Prayer*

Offering neither quick fixes nor canned prayers, this book links the spiritual disciplines of Bible study and prayer into one powerful tool to deepen your relationship with God.

In *Praying the Attributes of God,* Rosemary Jensen has compiled thirty-one prayer devotionals designed to direct thoughtful meditation on specific attributes of God, such as His accessibility, eternality, justice, holiness, and wisdom. Each short study highlights a divine attribute by using the ACTS acrostic, encompassing the four essential elements of a growing prayer life—Adoration, Confession, Thanksgiving, Supplication.

This guide is sure to enrich and revitalize your prayer life as you meditate on and respond to the truth of who God is in a focused way.